STORY DRAMAS

A New Literature Experience for Young Children

by Sarah Jossart & Gretchen Courtney

D1127020

Good Year Books

An Imprint of Addison-Wesley Educational Publishers, Inc.

ACKNOWLEDGMENTS

We would like to express a very sincere thank-you to Dr. Karen Pinter for her encouragement in this project. We also want to thank all the boys and girls who provided us with drama responses. With gratitude and love, we thank our families for their support.

 Good Year Books

are available for most basic curriculum subjects plus many enrichment areas. For more Good Year Books, contact your local bookseller or educational dealer. For a complete catalog with information about other Good Year Books, please write:

Good Year Books
1900 East Lake Avenue
Glenview, IL 60025

Book design by Meyers Design.

TABLE OF CONTENTS

From Story Dramas, published by Good Year Books. Copyright © 1997 Sarah Jossart & Gretchen Courtney.

FOREWORD

Dear Colleague,

We have written this book to get you started with story drama. Section 1, titled **Introduction to Story Drama,** explains what story drama is and a little about what to expect in a story drama experience by walking you through a sample drama and the follow-up exercises. We then show you the strong connection between story drama and reading instruction and how story drama can enhance your overall curriculum.

Section 2 includes **Warm-up Activities** to relax the students and to stimulate the imagination. The warm-ups help students who have never been exposed to drama, as well as those who have, but not in this environment (i.e., in this class, with these classmates).

The most exciting section is Section 3, **Story Dramas.** We start off with some helpful hints we have learned along the way, and then give you actual dramas compiled by genre: Poetry, Concept, Fantasy, Fiction, and Historical Fiction. The story dramas created for this book have been developed with some of our favorite pieces of literature, and each has proven to be a great success. Use them as is or use them as guides and adapt them to your liking. The teacher's spoken parts are boxed for your convenience. You can say the lines as printed, preview them and ad-lib, or redesign them yourself. We recommend you try a few of these dramas as models before you create your own. The books that accompany the dramas in this manual are easily found in your school or public library, or maybe on your own bookshelf.

After the actual story dramas is Section 4, **Step-by-Step: How to Construct Your Own Dramas.** This section will help you create your own dramas from your favorite pieces of literature. A discussion of writing extensions as part of story drama is presented next and a variety of writing ideas are shared.

Whether you are a librarian; a classroom teacher; or a gifted, reading, or special-education specialist, the story dramas in this book or the story dramas you might develop on your own are sure to be a pleasure for you and your students. Each time we have "dramatized" a story with students it is a new experience, for no two dramas develop in the same way.

We can honestly say students and teacher will emerge from a story drama experience saying, "Wow! That was really something!" So take on a role of a newspaper reporter or newcomer to town and visit Hokey Pokey Swamp. You'll be surprised at whom you might meet and from whence they came. Develop a problem or situation to solve, and the possibilities shared will be out of this world!

Enjoy,

Sarah and Gretchen
The Authors

From *Story Dramas*, published by Good Year Books. Copyright © 1997 Sarah Jossart & Gretchen Courtney.

INTRODUCTION TO STORY DRAMA

- **DEFINITION OF STORY DRAMA**

- **A STORY DRAMA EXAMPLE BASED ON "HUMPTY DUMPTY"**

- **EXAMPLES OF FOLLOW-UP ACTIVITIES**

- **THE CONNECTION BETWEEN DRAMA AND READING INSTRUCTION**

- **HOW STORY DRAMAS ENHANCE YOUR OVERALL CURRICULUM**

From *Story Dramas*, published by Good Year Books. Copyright © 1997 Sarah Jossart & Gretchen Courtney.

DEFINITION OF STORY DRAMA

Story drama allows students to become active participants in the stories and poems they hear and read. The written text—whether poetry, fiction, fantasy, or history—is the spark from which the students can begin to improvise, expand, and explore. The written text comes alive as students become characters within the text or create new characters. The expansion and exploration is accomplished through imagery, problem-solving, questioning, writing, art, and even cooking. Through these expansions and explorations of text, students have a deeper understanding of all the elements of literature. Through visualization of the story, the students see the literature coming alive.

The teacher/leader provides the following functions:

- Guides the students through the development of the drama by reading and then stopping at appropriate places in the text to allow the students the chance to explore and expand
- Models new situations, characters, feelings, and observations
- Models various questioning techniques, including open-ended questions expanding on students' ideas and text
- Establishes a problem to be solved within the context of the story and leads the students into the integration of the problem to real-life situations
- Models the acceptance of all ideas and guides the students into this acceptance
- Encourages every student to share and leads all students into active involvement
- Plays a role/character along with the students

The familiar nursery rhyme "Humpty Dumpty" is one of the simplest drama guides in this book. It is a good example of how poems and stories can be expanded into story dramas.

A STORY DRAMA EXAMPLE BASED ON "HUMPTY DUMPTY"

TEACHER AS A PARK RANGER: Welcome to _____ (inserts school's name) Park. I am Ms. Woods, one of the park rangers. I go around the park checking to make sure this is a safe place for all of us to be. It is nice to have you all in the park today. It is always more fun to know the other people who are with us in the park. Let's meet our new friends. Tell us your name, why you are in the park, and what you like about this park.

The teacher sets the stage for the drama. The only scripts are the teacher's roles, which the teacher is encouraged to ad-lib. The teacher models an introduction of his/her character.

Students should then introduce themselves in character to the group.

The students are quickly active participants. They are speaking and listening as well as creating their drama characters.

TEACHER AS MS. WOODS: Yesterday afternoon when you were all at _____ Park the most unusual thing happened. I understand you were all witnesses to an accident in the park. Just to remind you of the situation, I will read to you the accident report before I ask you some questions about what you saw happen.

> Humpty Dumpty sat on a wall.
> Humpty Dumpty had a great fall.
> All the king's horses and all the king's men,
> Couldn't put Humpty Dumpty back together again.

When the teacher reads the text, the text becomes "alive" as the students and teacher recall the event, which sparks the imagination of the drama.

TEACHER AS MS. WOODS (questioning the students in their roles):

What exactly did you see happen?

What exactly did you hear?

Where was Humpty Dumpty sitting? How high was the wall?

What was he doing up on the wall?

Should Humpty have known he should not be on that wall?

How would he have known this?

Who was Humpty Dumpty with?

Did any of you speak to him, and what did you say?

What did you do after the accident? How did you help?

What did you observe the king's men trying to do?

Do you have any other suggestions for them to try?

Will they work? Why or why not?

From *Story Dramas*, published by Good Year Books. Copyright © 1997 Sarah Jossart & Gretchen Courtney.

The teacher models questioning, and through questioning, the text is expanded and explored. Often a response will spark a new question. The list of questions is only the beginning of what might be discussed during a questioning part of the drama. The open-ended questions give all students the chance to continue participating in the drama. Accept all responses, allowing students to take risks and stay involved. Pay close attention to the roles students choose. Ask specific questions to them in these roles. For example, some students may have chosen to be police officers. What would they say to Humpty Dumpty? How would a mother or the park gardener help? Encourage students to ask questions of Ms. Woods and other characters concerning the accident.

Give students authentic chances to practice their questioning skills, and allow them the chance to expand on their ideas or their drama role.

TEACHER AS MS. WOODS: We want to make _____ Park a very safe place for everyone. Let's make a list of safety rules to post by the park entrance *(school playground)* so everyone remembers how to be safe.

A problem to be solved is presented to the group. The presentation of a problem gives the students practice in applying problem-solving techniques. Here students can apply past experiences, discuss cause and effect, and do some critical thinking.

Students in small groups make a list of safety rules. Each group shares their list. Then the class can compile a list of safety rules and post it near the exit to the school's playground.

Students are involved in both large- and small-group interaction during the drama. They are writing for an authentic purpose. They are learning and applying cooperative group decision-making skills. Posting or displaying student-generated responses tells the students of their worth as human beings.

EXAMPLES OF FOLLOW-UP ACTIVITIES
Ask students to
- Write a "get-well" letter to Humpty Dumpty.
- Write a newspaper account of this accident.
- Draw a picture showing what Humpty Dumpty was doing on the wall.
- Write a journal account of what they saw happening the day of the accident.
- Write about a favorite park.
- Draw a picture of what they like to do in the park.

From *Story Dramas*, published by Good Year Books. Copyright © 1997 Sarah Jossart & Gretchen Courtney.

Several follow-up activities are suggested. The students are asked to write, illustrate, cook, perform, and so on. These activities cover a wide range of expectations and are not labeled for a specific grade level or age span. Each teacher is free to select the activity or activities appropriate for his or her group of students. Select what you know your students can do, or possibly allow students an opportunity to select their own activities. This can allow for a wide range of abilities, from those of students in special education classes to the gifted. Don't be afraid to try a new activity! Model the activity, then work through the new activity as a group. As you stretch and challenge these young readers and writers, you will be amazed at what they can do.

Risk-taking will be a real part of a story drama experience, and students may need to participate in a couple of dramas before all students are willing to take the risks. Extended modeling of the teacher's roles will greatly enhance the students' performances. Be a risk-taker yourself. Warm-up activities before a drama will help students become more comfortable with the drama experience. Use the ideas for warm-ups in Section 2, Warm-ups.

THE CONNECTION BETWEEN DRAMA AND READING INSTRUCTION

Imagine—it is Tuesday morning, 9:15. According to your schedule, it is reading instruction time, and your students are playing the roles of exotic birds parading around the room. You, the teacher in the role of a toucan, are also parading. The door opens and in walks your principal. "What are you doing in here?" Just responding "Story drama" might give you an unwelcome frown, and we don't want any ruffled feathers, do we? So . . . what do you say?

Story drama is reading instruction. Students are listening to and reading some of the best of children's literature, including poetry, concept books, fantasy, fiction, and historical texts.

Story drama integrates writing activities. Students are given opportunities to write for many different reasons and audiences. Writing will happen during some dramas or as an extension of others.

Story drama is vocabulary development. Students are given the chance to hear new and cross-cultural vocabulary over and over again. Students are also given the chance to try out new words in real conversations through interaction in small-group or class discussions. All this exposure to new words and ways to use words helps students to incorporate new vocabulary into their own language.

Story drama is understanding a character's point of view as students play the roles of story characters or roles of other characters that could be part of a story.

Story drama is working with main idea, plot, and theme. Story text becomes real as students involve themselves in roles and problems to be solved.

Story drama is questioning and answering. Students generate their own questions as they interview each other about the characters they are playing or ask questions of a story character. Students make inferences, draw conclusions, compare and contrast, and evaluate as they answer questions posed to them. Many chances to ask and answer open-ended questions are all a part of story drama.

Story drama is a lesson in prediction. Students predict character roles, solutions to problems, and story outcomes.

By now you are out of breath and your principal is grinning from ear to ear. Your principal has spread her arms and asks, "May I join your parade?" Without a moment of hesitation you continue the story drama and provide reading instruction, as well as teach skills that favorably impact your overall curriculum.

HOW STORY DRAMAS ENHANCE YOUR OVERALL CURRICULUM

Story drama is schema-based instruction. Students are required to use prior knowledge and information to participate in character roles and problem-solving situations. Many times the problem to be solved is related to real-life situations, and students relate to those problems with knowledge they bring to the situation.

Story drama is acting, pretending, role-playing, dramatization, mime, and pantomime. Ideas generated by the students are performed or presented before the group or in small groups, giving students a variety of experiences.

Story drama is sharing. Ideas, introductions, problem solutions, dramatizations, and writings are all shared with small groups or with the whole class.

From *Story Dramas*, published by Good Year Books. Copyright © 1997 Sarah Jossart & Gretchen Courtney.

Story drama is a medium for reaching all students at all learning levels, whether they are strong in verbal, auditory, or hands-on skills. Each student can feel successful, and, therefore, learn. Group activities, in particular, allow students to share their special strengths and feel they have participated.

The current trend is to include students with diverse needs in regular classrooms. Story drama is particularly good at providing opportunities for all age levels and learning styles. Many students learn best in nontraditional ways, especially when the emphasis is placed on the development of critical thinking skills. In a story drama experience, all students will improve their ability to think critically, communicate effectively, and solve problems.

Story drama enhances imagination and creativity by allowing for opportunities to develop new characters, problem solve, and respond through illustrations and writing.

Story drama gives students a sense of belonging by involving them in activities in pairs, small groups, and large groups.

Story drama contributes to social growth by the teacher's acceptance of all student responses, and validation that all responses are valued as part of the community effort.

Story drama helps students see the teacher in a new light by observing the teacher participating in drama roles and play-acting with students. The teacher becomes more approachable.

SECTION 2

WARM-UPS

- **EXAMPLES OF WARM-UP ACTIVITIES**

- **ECHO PANTOMIME WARM-UPS**
  - "Goldilocks and the Three Bears"
  - "Three Billy Goats"
  - "Little Boy Blue"

- **NURSERY RHYME DRAMA WARM-UPS**
  - "Rub-a-dub-dub"
  - "There Was an Old Woman"
    (See Section 1 for "Humpty Dumpty" drama warm-up)

Warm-ups are very important if your group has not had many experiences in creative dramatics. Warm-up activities allow the students time to become risk-takers. Through warm-up activities students experience the open-ended expectations of the drama. Warming up for a few minutes is time well spent in that it helps your students become comfortable.

Begin by holding a discussion on pretending by asking these questions: How many of you have pretended? (Make sure you raise your hand too. Confirm that at one time or another everyone has pretended.) What have you pretended to do? Who or what have you pretended to be? Where have you pretended to be? As students share answers to these questions, point out that their examples show they have pretended to be different characters, imagined they are in various settings, and pretended to do a range of actions. Explain that pretending involves characters, setting, and action. We can pretend each separately or together in any combination.

After students are familiar with the concept of pretending, it may be helpful to remind them of the three ways of pretending before enacting each drama. It can also be to your advantage to inform the students before creating a drama which of the three types of pretending the drama will be asking them to do. For example, in "Humpty Dumpty," the example drama found in Section 1, the students pretend in character and setting.

EXAMPLES OF WARM-UP ACTIVITIES
Listed below are examples of activities to be used as warm-ups.

1. Have each student think of a favorite color. Have them do something with their hands and voice as they are saying the color to help convey the meaning of that color. For example, to illustrate the colors red and pink: Red—fan your face and say "Red" with an airy voice. Pink—move hands in a petting motion and say "Pink" in a soft voice. Try this also with a favorite animal or junk food.

2. Hand out an object (paper clip, clothes pin, bottle of glue, etc.). Then have small groups of students develop a story around this object and act it out.

From *Story Dramas*, published by Good Year Books. Copyright © 1997 Sarah Jossart & Gretchen Courtney.

3. Pantomime actions and see if students can identify what you are doing. For example:

> someone putting an ice cube down your back
> hitting your thumb with a hammer
> winning a lot of money
> riding a bike
> using a phone
> brushing your teeth
> getting pop out of a pop machine
> getting ready for school
> baking a cake
> making a bed
> taking a dog for a walk
> building a campfire
> fishing
> getting comfortable with a good book

4. Make noises for animals, people, and machines.

5. Make faces to show different expressions.

6. Move the body through different movements: stretch, become like a board, show your strength, and so on.

7. Have students close their eyes and imagine a birthday party, a favorite person coming to visit, petting a kitten, and so on. You may lead them through a guided imagery by giving them phrases to imagine. For example: You see a big birthday cake in the shape of a football, the chocolate frosting dripping onto the plate, the candles are burning lower and lower, you think of a wish, you blow out the candles, you hear them singing to you, and so on.

8. Many books lend themselves to warm-up activities. Along with the reading of the text, the students can pantomime actions and make appropriate noises. The following list of books is suggested:

> "Paddle," Said the Swan, by Gloria Kamen
> Read-Aloud Rhymes for the Very Young, selected by Jack Prelutsky
> Finger Rhymes, by Marc Brown
> Quick as a Cricket, by Audrey Wood
> A Farmyard Fiasco, by Dorothy Butler
> Farmer Duck, by Martin Widely
> In a Cabin in a Wood, adapted by Darcie McNally

9. Echo pantomimes and nursery rhymes make excellent warm-ups. Try one or more of those described in this chapter.

ECHO PANTOMIME WARM-UPS

"Goldilocks and the Three Bears" (retelling)
Echo Pantomime

Students echo each line after the teacher and imitate the actions demonstrated.

Teacher reads aloud and students echo:	Teacher demonstrates and students imitate:
Once upon a time	point to "watch" on wrist
there was a little girl named Goldilocks	twirl fingers by ears
One day, Goldilocks decides to go for a walk.	walk in place
She walks and walks	walk in place
deep into the forest.	put hands over eyes to shade
Suddenly Goldilocks sees a house.	open eyes wide
She peeks in the window.	put hands up to cup eyes
She knocks.	knocking motion
No one answers.	shake head side to side
Goldilocks tiptoes into the house.	tiptoe
She smells porridge.	sniff
She tries the big bowl.	pretend to eat
It's too hot.	fan hand across mouth
She tries the middle bowl.	pretend to eat
It's too cold.	shiver
She tries the little bowl,	pretend to eat
and she eats it all up.	rub stomach
Goldilocks decides to rest.	yawn
She tries this chair,	point
and this chair,	point in another direction
and that chair.	clap hands together for crash
Goldilocks tiptoes upstairs.	tiptoe
She sees three beds.	hold up three fingers
The first is too hard.	rub back
The second is too soft.	go limp
The third is just right.	make OK sign with fingers
And she falls asleep.	puts hands on side of head as if asleep

From *Story Dramas*, published by Good Year Books. Copyright © 1997 Sarah Jossart & Gretchen Courtney.

Teacher folds arms and pauses to say: Now we all know who really lives in this house.
Students respond: Who?

The three bears	hold up three fingers
see their porridge.	make sad faces
They see their chairs	wring hands
They see their beds.	shake head side to side
And they see Goldilocks	put hands up in the air
Goldilocks sees the bears.	make big eyes with fingers
She runs down the stairs,	run in place
out the door,	clap hands together for slam
and all the way home.	pant as if out of breath

"Three Billy Goats" (retelling)
Echo Pantomime

Students echo each line after the teacher and imitate the actions demonstrated.

Teacher reads aloud and students echo:	Teacher demonstrates and students imitate:
Once upon a time	fan your hands across face
there were three goats	hold up three fingers
and they were very hungry.	rub stomach
They could see green grass across the bridge.	hold hands as if looking out
"Let's go across the bridge" they said.	motion as if to follow
The Little Billy Goat started across the bridge.	measure "little" with fingers and walk in place
A mean ugly troll lived under the bridge.	scowl and talk roughly
He heard the trip trap of the Little Billy Goat.	cup ear
"Who's trip trapping across my bridge?"	cup mouth
"It is I, the Little Billy Goat."	measure "little" with fingers
"I'm going to gobble you up," said the troll.	move hands as if eating
"Oh no, please don't eat me.	fold hands

Wait for the Middle Size Goat, he's
   much bigger." ....push hands out in front of body
"Be gone with you." ....use hands to "wave off"
Then the troll heard the trip trap
   of the Middle Size Goat. ....cup ear
"Who's trip trapping across
   my bridge?" ....cup mouth
"It is I, the Middle Size Goat." ....spread out hands
"I'm going to gobble you up,"
   said the troll...move hands as if eating
"Oh no, please don't eat me. ....fold hands
Wait for the Biggest Billy Goat."................push hands out in front of you
"Be gone with you." ....use hands to "wave off"
Then the troll heard the trip trap
   of the Biggest Billy Goat. ....cup ear
"Who's trip trapping across
   my bridge?" ....cup mouth
"It is I, the Biggest Billy Goat." ....stretch
"I'm going to gobble you up,"
   said the troll...move hands as if eating
"Well come along," said the
   Biggest Billy Goat. ....motion as if to follow
Up came the mean ugly troll......................move feet as if climbing
The Biggest Billy Goat knocked
   the troll down. ....make fist
And that was the last of the
   mean ugly troll. ....wave "good-bye"
The Biggest Billy Goat went over
   to the green grass....................................walk in place
The three billy goats ate and ate................move hands as if eating
And they got very fat indeed.....................puff out chest and cheeks

"Little Boy Blue" (nursery rhyme)
Echo Pantomime

Students echo each line after the teacher and imitate the actions demonstrated.

Teacher reads aloud and students echo:	Teacher demonstrates and students imitate:
Little Boy Blue	show inch size with fingers
Come blow your horn.	form horn over mouth

From *Story Dramas,* published by Good Year Books. Copyright © 1997 Sarah Jossart & Gretchen Courtney.

The sheep's in the meadow ....hand over eyes as if looking

The cow's in the corn..................................put hand in back as tail

Where is the boy...place hands over eyes as if looking

Who looks after the sheep?..........................move head side to side

He's under the haystack................................bend as if to look under

Fast asleep. ....hands on side of face as if sleeping

Will you wake him? ....point to student

No, not I...point to self

For, if I do ....move hands out to sides

He's sure to cry. ....rub eyes

NURSERY RHYME DRAMA WARM-UPS

"Rub-a-dub-dub"
Nursery Rhyme Drama

Put students into groups of three. In these small groups they are to decide on what they might do if the three of them were together. The activity needs to be something that three can do.

Let each group share what they have decided would be a good activity for three people.

> **TEACHER AS NARRATOR:** I once read about a time, a long time ago, that a group of three men were in a wooden tub floating out to sea. As I recall, the tub was not very large, and it was the type you might have used to wash clothes in a long time ago. In your groups of three, pretend you are in this small wooden tub and seat yourself in a position you would take in the tub.

Ask students in each group to introduce themselves to the others in their group, tell their names, where they live, what they do for a living, and how they came about being in the tub.

Ask for volunteers to introduce the people in their tub, telling as much information as they can about what they have learned. Explore what problems they might face being in a tub at sea. List these problems on the board, and then brainstorm ways to solve each problem listed.

> **TEACHER AS NARRATOR** *(reading the poem aloud to the class):*
>   Rub-a-dub-dub
>   Three men in a tub.
>   And who do you think they be?
>   The butcher, the baker,
>   The candlestick-maker
>   And all of them gone to sea.

"There Was an Old Woman"
Nursery Rhyme Drama

Teacher plays the role of a reporter sent to the students' neighborhood to write a news story. Before writing the story you, as the reporter, want to get to know the neighborhood.

> **TEACHER AS NEWS REPORTER:** Good morning, I am a news reporter for the _____ *(local newspaper).* I have been sent to your neighborhood to write a follow-up to a news story. Before writing the story, I want to get to know you, the people of the neighborhood.

Students play the role of the neighbors. Ask for volunteers to introduce themselves. Have them tell who they are and what they do.

> **TEACHER AS NEWS REPORTER** *(questioning students in their roles):*
>   How long have you lived in this neighborhood?
>   What is the name of this street?
>   Have you always lived here?
>   Do you have any unusual neighbors or unusual things happening in your neighborhood?

Teacher reads aloud to the class the following poem. You might want to put the poem in a newspaper and read it as a news report.

From *Story Dramas*, published by Good Year Books. Copyright © 1997 Sarah Jossart & Gretchen Courtney.

TEACHER AS NARRATOR *(reading the poem aloud to the class):*

There was an old woman who lived in a shoe.

She had so many children she didn't know what to do.

She gave them some broth without any bread;

She whipped them all soundly and put them to bed.

TEACHER AS NEWS REPORTER *(continuing to question students in their roles):*

Do you know this neighbor? Could someone point out her home? Could you give me directions to this house?

What do you see as the problem? Have you offered to help? How did you help?

What have you observed going on at the old woman's house? Have any of you talked to the old woman? What did she have to say? What questions would you like to ask her?

How many children have you seen? Do you allow your children to play with her children? Why or why not? Where did all her children come from? Do you know if her children are being fed properly? Do you think they have enough clothing? Have the children caused problems in the neighborhood? If so, what have they done?

Put the students into groups of three. They will need to decide what is the most urgent problem and come up with a solution to the problem. (Examples might be children getting only broth to eat, getting spanked, or being too crowded in the shoe, or the old woman not knowing what to do.)

Small groups share their problems and solutions with the whole class. Discuss whether the ideas will work or why they might not work. Expand on the students' ideas.

FOLLOW-UP ACTIVITIES

Ask students to

- Write a group letter or individual letters to the old woman, explaining what should be done to help her or the children, depending upon the problem.
- Collect the letters. You might then step out of the room for a moment and return as the old woman (wearing a shawl, glasses, old hat, etc.). Read the letters to the group and respond to their suggestions. Give the students time to ask questions of the old woman.

SECTION 3

STORY DRAMAS

- **HINTS FOR SUCCESSFUL DRAMATIZING**

- **35 ACTUAL STORY DRAMAS CATEGORIZED BY GENRE**

  - Poetry

  - Concept

  - Fantasy

  - Fiction

  - Historical Fiction

HINTS FOR SUCCESSFUL DRAMATIZING

A List of Tips to Help You Engage Children in the Story Dramas

- Remember which character roles students are playing so you can go back to that "character" for questioning, problem solving, and so on.
- Use name tags for characters so you can call each character by name.
- Always plan to reread the story, poem, or drama text aloud for the students' enjoyment without the interruptions of the drama activity.
- Make provisions for the somewhat higher noise level associated with a successful story drama. (Remember you want your students to be actively involved using language.)
- Accept all responses. You may need to ignore an extreme student's responses by going on to another student.
- Do take time for a warm-up activity.
- Look for easy props such as caps, masks, and shirts.
- Use self-stick notes throughout the book to remind you where to stop. A few notes to yourself will help you remember the roles being played and questions you will be asking.
- Establish with the group the boundaries of the drama by letting them know what they are pretending: character, setting, or actions. This is a good way to establish the limits when playing action characters, aliens, and animals, unless these are clear within the limits of the drama.
- Story drama is versatile enough to be used in many other situations other than single-grade classrooms. Consider combining classes, putting on a whole-school drama, or asking parents to participate in a story drama on Parents' Night.
- Become familiar with the roles you, the teacher, will be playing so you can ad-lib these parts. Expand on these roles to become the character you want to be.
- Connect the drama activity with theme-centered units of study.
- When pages are not numbered, number them starting with the first page of text (unless noted otherwise in drama).

From *Story Dramas*, published by Good Year Books. Copyright © 1997 Sarah Jossart & Gretchen Courtney.

35 ACTUAL STORY DRAMAS CATEGORIZED BY GENRE

GENRE

POETRY

The reading of poetry is a great way to play around with language, especially the similar sounds in rhyming words. Poetry is full of visual imagery and imagination. Poem dramas are usually shorter than other types of dramas and provide for a variety of experiences. These experiences include exposure to a wide range of settings, emotions, subjects, and moods. Poetry offers many opportunities to become characters, solve problems, and create dramas.

During a drama, the text is read aloud to students. Poetry is written to be read aloud, and this is the best way to introduce students to the genre. As you question the students during a drama experience, you provide the opportunity to respond to the emotions, imagery, and subject matter of the poem.

There is an abundance of poetry available, including poems suitable for almost any content area and theme-centered unit. Planning a drama activity around a poem enhances and supports your curriculum.

The school-based poems found in *Mrs. Cole on an Onion Roll* should be especially interesting to students, who can easily dramatize, create characters, and become a part of the text when the setting is so familiar.

STORY DRAMA

"MRS. COLE ON AN ONION ROLL"

Based on the poem in Mrs. Cole on an Onion Roll
by Kalli Dakos
(Couplet poetry with real and make-believe foods)

> **TEACHER AS MRS. SPRATT:** I am Jack Spratt's wife, Samantha Spratt. It is so nice to meet all of you. I have just been hired by your school as the new lunch cook. I will be making all of your favorites. Today's specialty is spaghetti with prunes, pumpkin waffles, and zucchini cupcakes. I am very sorry that lunch is so late. Oh my, is it really 1:30? Let me hurry back to the kitchen and finish up.

From *Story Dramas*, published by Good Year Books. Copyright © 1997 Sarah Jossart & Gretchen Courtney.

Divide students up into small groups and have them come up with ways to let Samantha Spratt know what their favorite foods really are so that she may prepare them. Ask the students to write down ways to get the lunch menu changed in the future. Have the students also create a list of their favorite foods.

After the groups have discussed and written their solutions and lists, discuss the possible solutions as a group and decide upon the best method.

> **TEACHER AS NARRATOR:** Here comes Mrs. Spratt and your lunch. This is a good time to put your plan into action.

> **TEACHER AS MRS. SPRATT:** Well, well, you must be hungry. What, what's that? You want to tell or show me something? Very well, go on now.

The drama concludes with a role-play between one student, several students, or the entire class and Mrs. Spratt, enacting the solution to the food problem.

Read aloud the poem "Mrs. Cole on an Onion Roll."

FOLLOW-UP ACTIVITY

Ask students to switch their lists of favorite foods with another group. They should then use the foods on their lists to write couplets like those in the poem (the first line, a food from the list; the second line, a less desirable item to eat). They can illustrate or make murals illustrating their poetry creations.

a chocolate pie	hot dogs
cat guts	salad
chicken	pizza
slime	liver
squash	ice cream
eye balls	worms

From *Story Dramas*, published by Good Year Books. Copyright © 1997 Sarah Jossart & Gretchen Courtney.

STORY DRAMA

"FROG-A-LERT"

Based on the poem in Mrs. Cole on an Onion Roll
by Kalli Dakos
(Poem for the lover of creepy crawlies)

This drama incorporates the use of a powerful reading comprehension tool—visual imagery. Reading nonfiction books about insects, frogs, spiders, and so on, helps set the stage for this performance. The setting for this drama is April Fool's Day, but it could easily be adapted to fit the Halloween mood.

> **TEACHER:** Welcome to the first annual April Fool's contest. The category selected for this year's entries is "What can you bring to school in your pocket to scare the teacher?" You have all come here today with your entry—a pocket-sized surprise for fooling and fun. Everyone reach into your pocket. Feel your surprise. Is it bumpy, smooth, crusty, or slippery? Run your fingers over it and think about how it feels. Try to imagine what it looks like in your pocket. Is it colorful, dull, shimmery, or scaly? What does it smell like?

stiky
farry
but
smushy
green blue
ets flys

Hand the students a piece of paper folded in half. Instruct students to draw a picture of what they have in their pocket on the inside of the paper and write a description of what it looks, feels, and smells like on the outside of the paper.

Divide the class into partners or small groups. Taking turns, have each student read or recite his or her description and have the partner or other group members guess what is in the speaker's pocket.

Read aloud the poem "Frog-a-lert."

FOLLOW-UP ACTIVITY

- Ask students to rewrite this poem, making it "Bug-a-lert," "Spider-a-lert," and so on. Have them read their new versions aloud to enjoy the sounds and rhythms of language.

STORY DRAMA
"I LOST MY TOOTH IN MY DOUGHNUT"

Based on the poem in Mrs. Cole on an Onion Roll
by Kalli Dakos
(Portrays an important youthful event)

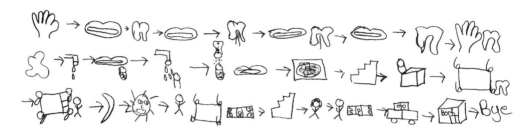

Read aloud the poem "I Lost My Tooth in My Doughnut" to the class. Create a class chart listing all the ways that the students have lost teeth. Share and enjoy all the tooth-pulling tales from the students.

TEACHER AS THE DIRECTOR OF THE TOOTH-FAIRY TRAINING FACILITY: Welcome, welcome, beginning tooth fairies. You are going to spend the next four days learning all of the things that tooth fairies must do. You have been chosen from hundreds of other young people to be tooth fairies. This is a very important job. I am sure you will do well. Now, tell us how you were chosen to be a tooth fairy.

   Who selected you for this important job?
   What will you have to learn?
   Will this job be difficult? Why or why not?
   Do you know any other tooth fairies? Who are they?

It has come to my attention that many young students are pulling out their teeth the wrong way, causing much pain and tears. The Tooth Fairy Association is going to send a step-by-step, tooth-pulling instruction manual to each student on his or her fourth birthday. Our job is to decide what are the best steps to take when pulling a tooth and write them down for the instruction manual.

As a class, create a how-to manual for tooth pulling. Include instructions for holding the tooth, types of pulling techniques, ways to stop the bleeding, and so on.

From *Story Dramas*, published by Good Year Books. Copyright © 1997 Sarah Jossart & Gretchen Courtney.

FOLLOW-UP ACTIVITIES

Ask students to

- Listen to a rereading of the poem "I Lost My Tooth in My Doughnut" and the letters to and from the tooth fairy found on the same page. Then have them write their own letters to the tooth fairy.
- Tell about their own first lost tooth, or if it hasn't happened yet, interview someone and tell his or her story (a parent, sibling, baby-sitter, etc.).
- Write a group letter to the tooth fairy, asking her how she knows when a tooth is lost and how she decides what amount of money the tooth is worth.

STORY DRAMA

"ME"

Based on the poem in My Song Is Beautiful
selected by Mary Ann Hoberman
poem by Karla Kuskin
(A child's description of himself)

TEACHER AS MRS. PIFFLE: Welcome, students. I am Mrs. Piffle. You are the very first young people to be allowed to come to the create-a-face factory. You can choose any type of face you want for yourself, and we can make it right here. You can even wear it home today! Please check in with me on your way into the factory. *(Asks students the following questions about themselves.)*

Who are you?

Why have you come to the create-a-face factory?

Do you think this will be expensive?

What do you think your friends will say when they see you looking different?

What will your mother or father say about the way you will look after you change your face?

How do you think the technicians in the factory go about changing the way you look?

Think about what you might like to change about the way you look. Do you want longer or shorter hair? What about your eyes—would you like a different color?

It is time to get started on our tour. Are you ready?

On a piece of paper divided into four sections, students should create a face. In one section of the paper, have them draw what they want their eyes to look like. Ask, "Do you want your eyes to look the same as they do now, or do you want them to look different?" In another section of their paper, have them draw what they want their hair to look like. Ask, "Is it just the way you want it to be, or could it be longer, shorter, curlier, or straighter?" In the other sections of their paper, have them draw two things they like about themselves. Ask volunteers to share their drawings with others.

TEACHER AS MRS. PIFFLE: Oh my! Something is terribly wrong! Our computers and machines are all going crazy. Somebody help! Oh dear, here comes one of our customers now!

Read aloud the poem "Me" to the class.

FOLLOW-UP ACTIVITIES
Ask students to
- Write a letter to someone they have never met, such as a pen pal. Include in the letter a description of themselves.
- Write down all the things they like about themselves.

STORY DRAMA

"I KNOW SOMEONE"

Based on the poem in My Song Is Beautiful
poem by Michael Rosen
(Describes the interesting things children do)

This drama encourages students to exhibit some of the "special talents" they can perform using their eyes, noses, arms, legs, and other movable body parts. All students have crazy things that they can perform, such as wiggling their ears or rolling their tongues, and they enjoy the opportunity to show their unusual talents to others.

Read aloud the poem "I Know Someone" to the class twice.

From *Story Dramas*, published by Good Year Books. Copyright © 1997 Sarah Jossart & Gretchen Courtney.

TEACHER AS DR. ZANTO: What excitement there is at _____ School! We are preparing for the first annual silly-trick contest. My name is Dr. Zanto and I am principal here. We will be preparing to put on the best silly-trick contest ever. All the students in this school are getting ready to perform one of these most amazing silly tricks, without props. Why, hello, class. I have stopped by to see what you are doing to get ready for the silly-trick contest. *(Asks the students the following questions.)*

> What is your name, and what class are you in?
>
> Are you excited about the silly-trick contest?
>
> What are you going to do as your trick?
>
> Do you have brothers and sisters participating in the contest?
>
> What are they going to do for the silly-trick contest?

Have students think about something special they can do with their mouths, ears, eyes, hands, feet, or other parts of their bodies that hardly anyone else can do. Ask them to draw a picture of themselves doing that trick, and then write the name of the trick on the bottom. These pictures should be hung up all over the school, advertising their performances at the silly-trick contest. (Ask students' permission to do this.)

I rolled my eyes.

TEACHER AS DR. ZANTO: Today is the big day! Today is the silly-trick contest that everyone in the school has worked so hard to prepare. I am judging the contest, and I know how difficult it will be to pick just one winner. I had better hurry down to the gym to get ready. I will see you there!

One by one, have students stand up, tell their names, and perform their silly tricks for the rest of the class.

TEACHER AS DR. ZANTO: Those were great! Everyone did a fabulous job, but I think the silliest trick was _____, done by _____. Thank you everyone for the great show. Now let's all stand up, and you can do your silly tricks again.

FOLLOW-UP ACTIVITY

- Have students ask their parents what silly tricks they or their relatives can do. Then ask them to show or tell the rest of the class about these tricks.

STORY DRAMA

"THE END"

Based on the poem in My Song Is Beautiful
poem by A. A. Milne
(Describes the first years of life)

Tell a story about one of your birthday celebrations from the years you were four, five, or six.

Read aloud the first stanza of the poem "The End."

Have students think back to what it was like when they were babies. Ask them what one-year-old children can and cannot do. Have them pretend that someone has just put a big birthday cake in front of them with a single lit candle shining on the top. Then have them pantomime what they would do if they were only one year old.

Read aloud the rest of the poem.

Have students form small groups and plan what they think would be the best birthday party ever. Have each group write a guest list, decide where the party will be, where they will go, and what they will do for fun. After students have planned their parties, have them share their ideas with the rest of the class.

FOLLOW-UP ACTIVITY
• Ask students to write or draw their favorite birthday celebration.

STORY DRAMA

"A VISIT FROM ST. NICHOLAS"

Based on the poem also known as "'Twas the Night Before Christmas"
by Clement C. Moore
(A glimpse at the magic of Christmas)

"A Visit from St. Nicholas" is the age-old classic narrative poem, first printed in 1823, that most of us know as "Twas the Night Before Christmas." The poem describes an idyllic family setting on Christmas Eve, with mother and father settling into bed and the children fast asleep. During the night, St. Nicholas makes his visit, arriving by a sleigh drawn by eight flying reindeer. The tale is told by the father, who is lucky enough to catch a glimpse of the elusive St. Nick.

This poem drama extends the small family unit represented in the poem into a large family reunion. Students become part of this family, often portraying one of their own family members. The magic of Christmas adds excitement to this drama as the students tell each other which "sugar-plums" they are dreaming about. Further along in the drama, the students play the parts of Santa's reindeer. Students will enjoy this and give the reindeer many human characteristics, which will help them better understand the concept of personification.

Playing a recording of this poem before and after the drama is one more way of helping students fully enjoy this special seasonal drama.

TEACHER AS BOB NOEL: Welcome to the Noel family reunion. I am Bob Noel, and I have invited all of you, my relatives, to join my family and me in celebrating this Christmas holiday. I haven't seen many of you for years, and some of you I have never met. Let's get acquainted. *(Asks students to introduce themselves and tell a little bit about themselves: how old they are, where they have come from, how they are related to the Noel family, etc.)* Well, it is Christmas Eve here at the Noel house. We have just eaten a tremendous Christmas feast and now everyone is settling in for the night.

TEACHER AS NARRATOR (*reading aloud from poem*):

'Twas the night before Christmas and all through the house

Not a creature was stirring, not even a mouse;

The stockings were hung by the chimney with care,

In hopes that St. Nicholas soon would be there.

The children were nestled all snug in their beds,

While visions of sugar-plums danced in their heads.

TEACHER AS BOB NOEL: All of you are sleeping on sleeping bags together in our family room near the Christmas tree. Everyone is almost asleep and dreaming about sugar-plums. Turn to a relative close to you and tell them what you were dreaming about. Remember to whisper.

Good night everyone. We are going upstairs to bed. Let us know if you need anything.

TEACHER AS NARRATOR (*reading aloud from poem*):

And momma in her kerchief, and I in my cap,

Had just settled our brains for a long winter's nap,

When out on the lawn there arose such a clatter,

I sprang from my bed to see what was the matter.

Away to the window I flew like a flash,

Tore open the shutters and threw up the sash.

The moon on the breast of the new-fallen snow

Gave the luster of midday to objects below;

When, what to my wondering eyes should appear

But a miniature sleigh and eight tiny reindeer,

With a little old driver, so lively and quick,

I knew in a moment it must be St. Nick.

More rapid than eagles his coursers they came,

And he whistled, and shouted, and called them by name:

"Now, Dasher! now, Dancer! now, Prancer and Vixen!

On, Comet! on Cupid! on, Donner and Blitzen!

To the top of the porch! To the top of the wall!

Now, dash away! dash away! dash away all!

From *Story Dramas*, published by Good Year Books. Copyright © 1997 Sarah Jossart & Gretchen Courtney.

TEACHER AS REPORTER: Thank goodness I got here in time to get an exclusive TV interview with Santa and his reindeer. Oh my, let me introduce myself. My name is Merry Holiday, from XYZ-TV. I am new at the station, and I have been assigned to find Santa and his reindeer. Here we are at the Noel house. Santa has just disappeared down the chimney. I am standing next to the eight tiny reindeer. *(Students take the parts of the reindeer being interviewed by the reporter. Reporter asks the "reindeer" the following questions.)*

How did you get this job?

Do you work long hours?

What is the job like?

Are the benefits good?

What is Santa like to work for?

What do you do in the off season?

Thank you, Santa's reindeer, for letting me interview you. I am going to rush this back to the station for the 10:00 news.

TEACHER AS NARRATOR *(reading aloud from poem):*
As dry leaves that before the wild hurricane fly,
When they meet with an obstacle, mount to the sky,
So up to the housetop the coursers they flew,
With a sleigh full of toys, and St. Nicholas too.
And then in a twinkling, I heard on the roof
The prancing and pawing of each little hoof.

Santa is up on the roof now. Luckily the Noel family has a chimney. But Santa is having a big problem these days with the houses that don't have chimneys. As a matter of fact, he is running a contest to see who can come up with the best idea for what Santa should do to get into a house that doesn't have a chimney. The winner of this contest gets a trip to the North Pole to visit Santa's workshop.

Divide the class into groups of five or six and have them work together to come up with a good idea to enter in this contest. Have them write it down, and then have each group read their idea out loud to the rest of the class. Discuss the ideas with the whole group. Take a vote to determine a winner.

From *Story Dramas*, published by Good Year Books. Copyright © 1997 Sarah Jossart & Gretchen Courtney.

TEACHER AS NARRATOR (*reading aloud from poem*):

I drew in my head, and was turning around,

Down the chimney St. Nicholas came with a bound.

He was dressed all in fur from his head to his foot,

And his clothes were all tarnished with ashes and soot.

TEACHER AS BOB NOEL: Wake up everybody! Santa is coming down our chimney. What does he look like to you? Is he tall or short? What color are his eyes? How old do you think he is?

Have students draw pictures of the Santa they see coming out of the fireplace. After about five minutes, read the next part of the poem, encouraging students to add to their picture as they get new information.

TEACHER AS NARRATOR (*reading aloud from poem*):

A bundle of toys he had flung on his back,

And he looked like a peddler just opening his pack.

His eyes, how they twinkled! His dimples, how merry!

His cheeks were like roses, his nose like a cherry;

His droll little mouth was drawn up like a bow,

And the beard on his chin was as white as the snow.

The stump of a pipe he held tight in his teeth,

And the smoke, it encircled his head like a wreath.

He had a broad face, and a little round belly

That shook, when he laughed, like a bowl full of jelly.

He was chubby and plump—a right jolly old elf;

And I laughed, when I saw him, in spite of myself.

A wink of his eye, and a twist of his head,

Soon gave me to know I had nothing to dread.

He spoke not a word, but went straight to his work,

And filled all the stockings; then turned with a jerk,

And laying his finger aside of his nose,

And giving a nod, up the chimney he rose.

He sprang to his sleigh, to his team gave a whistle,

And away they all flew, like the down of a thistle.

But I heard him exclaim, ere he drove out of sight,

"Happy Christmas to all, and to all a good-night!"

From *Story Dramas*, published by Good Year Books. Copyright © 1997 Sarah Jossart & Gretchen Courtney.

TEACHER AS BOB NOEL: Well, this has been quite an exciting evening. Let's all try to get some sleep, and I will see all of you in the morning.

FOLLOW-UP ACTIVITIES

Ask students to

- Listen to a recording of the poem, "A Visit from St. Nicholas," after the drama. (You may want to pass out hard candy [sugar-plums] and have students eat their sugar-plums and finish their Santa drawings during the recording.)
- Design a Christmas stocking for the Noel family characters in this drama. The stocking should include the name each student gave himself or herself and some items that coincide with the student's personality. For example, if a student played a relative from Arizona, perhaps the stocking might have cactus designs on it.
- Write a thank-you note to the Noel family for sharing their Christmas with you.
- Write letters to each other, pretending that they have returned home and are writing to a relative that they met at the reunion.
- Compare several different examples of this poem illustrated by different artists. (One page that is especially interesting to compare is the page illustrating sugar-plums.)
- Listen to or read versions of this poem written by James Rice: *Cajun Night Before Christmas, Hillbilly Night Before Christmas, Cowboy Night Before Christmas* or *La noche buena South of the Border.*

STORY DRAMA

"SKYWRITING"

Based on the poem in the book Sky Words
by Marilyn Singer
(A plane is used to draw and write messages in the sky)

Two poetry dramas follow from *Sky Words*, but several other poems in this collection could be developed into dramas too: "December 31," "When the Tornado Came," and "In the City."

> **TEACHER AS MS. SPRATT:** Welcome to McGregor's Skywriting School. I am Ms. Spratt. I am one of the instructors for the school. I hear you folks have come from all over the world to learn skywriting. Some of you may be just learning how to skywrite, and some of you are here to learn more about it. Before we begin our instruction, it is always good to know the other students in our class.

Have students form pairs and introduce themselves to their partners. Suggest they tell who they are, where they came from, and then one thing they hope to learn at McGregor's Skywriting School.

As a group activity, have volunteers introduce their partners to others.

> **TEACHER AS MS. SPRATT** (*questioning students in their roles as they are introduced*):
>   Why do you want to learn _____? (*Inserts what they have said they want to learn at skywriting school.*)
>   When and where will you use this new learning?
>   For what occasions have you, or will you, write messages in the sky?
>   Do you fly alone? Why or why not?
>   What weather conditions must you have before you can fly?
>   Would you fly in rain? Why or why not?
>   Do you want to learn to print or do cursive writing in the air?
>   What advice can you experienced flyers give to us about skywriting?
>   Have you ever made a mistake skywriting? If so, what was your mistake?
>   Does anyone know how I can improve the dotting of an *i* when I skywrite?
>   What message would you write over a school, park, grocery store, or home?

From *Story Dramas*, published by Good Year Books. Copyright © 1997 Sarah Jossart & Gretchen Courtney.

Have students pretend to be skywriters. Ask if they have any questions for the instructor. What are they?

(Note to Teacher: If you are asked a question you cannot answer, the following responses work: I don't know that answer. I am still learning more and more about skywriting myself. Learning never seems to stop. I'm not sure of the answer. What do you think? Can you think of a way we could find the answer to that question? Who could we ask?)

Read poem aloud through the first six lines.

> **TEACHER AS MS. SPRATT:** Students of McGregor's Skywriting School, before we go up in the air to practice our writing, we must have in mind what we will be writing and how we might write these letters.

Students should brainstorm together ways to make letters, such as block, wavy, stick, cursive, dots, circle, and so on. Have students illustrate on the chalkboard these different ways of writing.

Have students think about the messages they will write. Remind them that these messages are short, and the words they select are very important to the message. These could be messages to the president, their city, or a special person, or they could be an advertisement for a company. Ask for several students to share their ideas and discuss. Rework messages together and list them on the board.

Read aloud lines 7–12 of the poem.

> **TEACHER AS MS. SPRATT:** Now students, select one message and think of a picture you would like to make to go with that message. Plan out a design for the picture and writing on a piece of paper. Decide how you want each letter to look and where you want the picture.

Have students write and draw their messages. Read aloud lines 13 through the end of the poem. Have students share their "skywritings."

> **TEACHER AS MS. SPRATT** *(asking the skywriters the following questions):*
> What would you do differently the next time you went skywriting?
> What went wrong with your plans?
> Are you going to keep practicing? Why or why not?

To end the drama experience, reread aloud the entire poem for everyone's enjoyment.

FOLLOW-UP ACTIVITIES
Ask students to
- Write a journal account of a real or imaginary plane ride.
- Draw a picture of what you think the gardener, cop, sunbather, baseman, and jackhammer man from the poem look like.
- Write a paragraph telling why they would like to be a pilot, or why not.

STORY DRAMA

"AT THE FAIR"

Based on the poem in the book Sky Words
by Marilyn Singer
(A day is spent at the fair)

In preparation for this drama, pass out "tickets" good for one ride at the fair. Tell the students that the ticket will be needed later in the day. Have ready a measuring line for students to use in measuring their heights; this might be a strip of paper or a simple line drawn on the chalkboard. Make the line short enough so all students do pass the height, but close enough so some of them might think they have to measure to check whether they are taller than the line.

From *Story Dramas*, published by Good Year Books. Copyright © 1997 Sarah Jossart & Gretchen Courtney.

TEACHER AS GREETER: Welcome to the fair. Get your tickets and be ready for a day at the fair.

Read aloud the first ten lines of the poem.

TEACHER AS THE TICKET TAKER: As the ticket agent, I must tell you I have some good news and some bad news. The ride is going today, but the line is very long, and I must warn you that the ride is scary. If you have heart problems or think you will faint, you need to leave the line. Also, if you do not think you are tall enough for this ride, please step up and measure yourself to make sure. *(Lets students measure.)* As I said, the line is very long, so to help the time pass let's have you get to know the other people in line with you. Ask someone near you his or her name, where he or she is from, and why he or she is going on this ride.

Students should interview partners and then introduce them to the rest of the group. Tell their names, where they are from, and why they are going on the ride.

TEACHER AS THE TICKET TAKER *(questioning students in their roles):*
  What scary rides have you been on before?
  What do you think makes this ride so scary?
  How long will you wait to go on this ride?
  How much would you pay to go on this ride?
  Do you know anyone that would not go on this ride? Why would they not go?
  How many rides have you been on already today?
  Will you keep your eyes open during the ride? Why or why not?
  Describe the ride as you see it from this line.

TEACHER AS THE TICKET TAKER: Ladies and gentlemen, this is your last chance to leave this ride. I need to tell you a little bit more about this ride. You will be riding alone. You will be in the dark, and when the ride starts the floor will drop. I will be coming around to collect your tickets. *(Walks around the room and picks up tickets.)* Settle back in your seats, fasten your seat belts, and check to make sure nothing is on the floor. Are you ready?

Read aloud lines 11–26 and pause.

> **TEACHER AS THE TICKET TAKER:** Ladies and gentlemen, your ride is over. Thank you for riding with us today. This is a new attraction here at the fair, and we are asking the first one hundred people who ride it to give us their comments. As you leave the ride please give one comment about the ride. *(Goes around the room asking for comments about the ride.)*

Read aloud line 27 through the end of the poem.

> **TEACHER AS THE TICKET TAKER** *(questioning students):*
> Will you go on that scary ride again?
> What will you do at the fair now?
> Who do you think would have enjoyed this special ride?
> What has been the best part about going to the fair?

Reread the poem with no interruptions.

FOLLOW-UP ACTIVITIES

Ask students to

- Give the ride in the poem a name, and then write or tell a descriptive account of their rides.
- Draw a picture of the ride in the poem and write a description of their drawings or make a list of descriptive words about their designs.
- Design an advertisement for a new ride at the fair.
- Write a group or individual note to a mother, trying to persuade her to go on the ride.
- Design a new ride and write a persuasive letter to the president of the park convincing him to purchase the ride.
- Write a report to the safety commission, persuading them that the ride is safe or unsafe.

From *Story Dramas*, published by Good Year Books. Copyright © 1997 Sarah Jossart & Gretchen Courtney.

GENRE

CONCEPT

Concept books are for the early years when students are curious about the world around them. These books explore the senses, colors, size differences, numbers, alphabet letters, and so on. Some concept books have little or no written story line but depend entirely upon conveying meaning through illustrations. Concept books give information by using what students already are familiar with and expanding on that knowledge. Using concept books with young students gives them the basis for seeing relationships between objects, concepts, and ideas.

STORY DRAMA

"PARADE"

Based on the book by Donald Crews
(A real parade)

The elements of a parade are presented in this concept book, but the best part of this story drama is the preparation for and the participation in a parade. Many students have seen parades on TV, but the "real" experience is something they might not have had.

When is the last time you participated in a parade? In this drama, your students will feel the excitement of anticipating a parade and the experience of participating in one.

Superman went to the parade.

Here are some preparation suggestions for before the drama experience. Depending upon the variation your class takes for the parade, the amount of supplies and type of supplies will vary. See the parade variations listed at the end of the drama text. Make these items available:

- Art supplies—colored construction paper, glue, crayons, markers, grocery bags, magazines for pictures, rolls of paper, and so on.
- Musical instruments—bells, triangle, drums, and so on.

Place students in two long rows facing each other. Leave a space between the rows for the "street" or "parade" route.

Read aloud the book through the page where the crowd is all lined up waiting for the parade. (Text pages are not numbered.)

TEACHER AS NEWS REPORTER: Welcome to the _____ (inserts school name) Parade. I am Ms. Speak from WYYT, Channel 7. I'm covering the _____ Parade. You have traveled from all over the world to watch this parade. We don't know each other, but we would like to know about you. Tell us your name, where you are from, what you enjoy the most about a parade, and why you are here for the _____ Parade. (Interviews students. Encourages students to introduce themselves. Asks these additional questions.)

What famous person do you hope to see in the parade? How will you know that person?

What vendors have you seen?

What souvenir will you buy?

What was the last parade you attended?

What do you expect to see in this parade?

Who came with you to the parade?

What song do you hope the band will be playing?

Will you see animals? Why or why not?

How long have you been waiting for the parade?

What do you think you will see first in the parade? Why?

From *Story Dramas*, published by Good Year Books. Copyright © 1997 Sarah Jossart & Gretchen Courtney.

> **TEACHER AS NARRATOR:** While we're waiting for the parade to start, I'd like to read to you about another parade.

Read aloud the text, skipping the page where the parade starts and going right to the next page with the flags. Read through to the page with the fire engine and stop.

> **TEACHER AS NEWS REPORTER:** That was a wonderful parade we read about in that book, but the parade we came to see today seems to be having some problems. I haven't seen it come down the street. *(Question students in their roles.)*
>
>   What do you think has happened to our _____ Parade?
>   What do you think we should do?
>   How are you feeling?
>   Are any of you going to go home? Why or why not?
>
> Just a minute folks, the TV station is trying to get my attention. The receiver in my ear is clicking, so I must listen to what they are telling me. *(Pauses and does sad facial expressions.)* Oh no! Folks, I'm sorry to announce the parade has been canceled. There seems to be a technical problem and no one knows how to fix it. *(Pauses again, as though another message is coming through. Do excited and happy facial expressions.)* The TV station now tells me that we can have our own parade, because the streets are clear. Let's plan a parade!

Students should begin planning their parade. Playing marching music in the background as they begin to plan will add to the anticipation of the parade.

From *Story Dramas*, published by Good Year Books. Copyright © 1997 Sarah Jossart & Gretchen Courtney.

PARADE VARIATIONS

1. Brainstorm with the class ideas for doing a parade. This will be open-ended and supplies for the parade decided upon will vary.

2. Divide the class into groups. Each group decides what it wants to be in the parade. Using the art supplies, each person in the group makes some kind of costume to represent his or her part in the parade. Ideas from the book might be used, but clowns, animals, and so on, could be added. General art supplies will be needed.

3. For a band parade, all the students are members of a marching band with a majorette. Each must design a "uniform" (grocery bag vests or vests cut from paper). The musical instruments would be used in this parade. This parade works well in kindergarten and first grade. Plan to coordinate this parade with the music teacher so the students know how to handle the instruments.

4. A parade could be planned around a holiday, content unit, or theme unit of study. The parade could be a culminating activity with each student designing something to wear or carry that goes with the holiday, unit of study, or theme.

PARADE HINTS

This activity works best if the students are aware of the amount of time they will have to plan and make their costume or the object they will be carrying. It can be done over a couple of days or within one time period.

FOLLOW-UP ACTIVITIES

Ask students to

- Write a group or individual account about the experience.
- Write a newspaper report covering the parade. This report would cover the who, what, when, where, why, and how questions.
- Design an advertisement for the upcoming parade.
- Write about what they might see or have seen in a parade.
- Draw pictures of themselves in the class parade and label the pictures.
- Take photographs of themselves in the parade and then bring the pictures home to their parents. Suggest they tell their parents about the parade.

From *Story Dramas*, published by Good Year Books. Copyright © 1997 Sarah Jossart & Gretchen Courtney.

STORY DRAMA

"A CHILDREN'S ZOO"

Based on the book by Tana Hoban
(A celebration of animals)

Penguins, hippopotami, zebras, and parrots waddle, swim, gallop, and squawk around the room in this introductory drama for young students. The only written text in this concept book is three descriptive words for each animal pictured. The sounds and movements of zoo animals are an excellent way for students to learn and practice using their bodies and voices as tools for creating characters in other dramas. There is a lot of movement and noise in this drama!

Once students have created all of the animals in the book, a simple situation is posed and students respond in their animal forms. Animals living in their natural habitat outside the zoo correspond with the animals inside the zoo, asking questions and exchanging tales and adventures. In this drama, the animals take on very interesting personalities!

To begin, read aloud the first page and show the color photograph on the second page. (The pages are not numbered; start numbering on the first page and number all pages.)

Have students stand up and pose their bodies to look like the penguin in the picture. Ask them to waddle around the room like a penguin and then waddle over to the zoo fence and look at all the people watching them at the zoo.

Read aloud the third page and show the color photograph on the fourth page.

Read aloud the fifth page and show the color photograph on the sixth page.

Have students change their bodies to look like the zebra in the picture. Ask them to gallop around the room like a zebra.

From *Story Dramas*, published by Good Year Books. Copyright © 1997 Sarah Jossart & Gretchen Courtney.

TEACHER AS NARRATOR (*asking the following questions of the zebras in the room*):

Were you born in this zoo or another zoo?

Are you living with your family? Who are they?

What do you think of the cage/fenced-in area where you live?

What are the zookeepers like?

What is it like to live in the zoo?

Read aloud the rest of the text pages and show all of the photographs. Stop at the lion page and the parrot page for the students to transform themselves into those animals.

Ask students to choose their favorite animal from this book. Have them think about what it is like for this animal to live in the zoo. Suggest they write a letter or draw a picture to send to one of their family members still living in the wild. (Note to the Teacher: The last page of text tells where the animals come from, what that area is like, and what they eat. This is a good reference page for students who do not have the background to start this assignment.)

After students draw their pictures or write their letters, have them sit with a partner and tell about what they have drawn or written. Then exchange drawings or letters and write or draw a reply to the drawing or letter they now have.

FOLLOW-UP ACTIVITIES

Ask students to

- Hang up drawings or letters so that others can write back.
- Write a group letter to a zoo asking how a particular animal in the book is cared for.
- Role-play a favorite animal in a "mini-drama," in which the animals get together after the people have gone home and the zookeepers are asleep.
- Make a "Zoo Book" using Tana Hoban's picture and three-word format.

STORY DRAMA

"CHICKA CHICKA BOOM BOOM"

Based on the book by Bill Martin, Jr., and John Archambault
(The characters are alphabet letters.)

The idea for this interesting alphabet concept book came from John Archambault's infant son, Arie Alexander Archambault. In Arie's room over his changing table hung an alphabet mobile. After hearing the alphabet recited over and over by his parents, Arie tried his own version, which sounded a great deal like "chicka chicka boom boom."

In this story, the alphabet letters are the characters. The capital letters are the adults and the small letters are the naughty children. Students create characters and solve problems in this drama, but the most fun is seeing the letters climb and tumble from the coconut tree.

TEACHER AS SMALL LETTER *d* *(singing the "ABC" song):* A-B-C—I love this song all about us letters. Little *d*, that's me, see—*(bending body into a shape resembling the small letter d).* D-d-d—what a great family I have. *D*'s are in such fun words as *noodle* and *poodle. Dad, David,* and *dictionary* have us *d*'s in them also. We are so tall and strong. My Dad—big *D*, is really tough. He is so BIG. He is bigger than almost all the other letters. Look around, all the alphabet is here today. I'm going to find my friend *p*.

TEACHER AS NARRATOR *(showing students the inside cover illustrating the alphabet):* Here is a picture of us. Which letter are you? What is special about your letter? Show us what you look like. *(Students use their bodies to create shapes.)* Describe yourself. Are you short and round, or tall and thin?

Read aloud the first and second pages of the book. (Pages are not numbered.)

Rope, Bricks, Stairs, Trampoline

> **TEACHER AS SMALL LETTER *d*:** I want to go too! I want to climb up the coconut tree! *(Questions students in their roles.)*
>
> What about all you other alphabet letters?
>
> Do you want to climb to the top of the coconut tree? Why or why not?
>
> Do you think we need to ask permission to climb the tree? Why or why not?
>
> Who should we ask for permission to climb this tree?

Divide students into groups according to their letters, for example, *aeou, kbdpq, gjy, cfhlt, imnv, rswxz.* Have students pretend they are the letters in their groups. Ask them how they will get to the top of the tree. Have them think about their shape. Ask how this shape can help them climb the tree. Ask how their shapes and sizes make it harder. Suggest students share their ideas with the rest of the class.

Read aloud pages 3–12. Show illustration on pages 11 and 12.

> **TEACHER AS SMALL LETTER *d*:** Ouch—quit pushing. Your dot is in my face. Little *t*—move to the side. I need to get out. I can't believe we all fell. What kind of tree is this? It can't even hold up alphabet letters.

Using their bodies, have students show how they are all stooped and jumbled in the pile.

Read aloud pages 13–26.

> **TEACHER AS DR. LETTERS:** I am Dr. Letters. My specialty is the care of young alphabet letters. We have just had a big accident at the coconut tree. The ambulances are bringing in some of the most injured letters now. Here comes the first case. *(Interviews a few students in their roles as injured letters.)*
>
> Which letter are you?
>
> What hurts?
>
> Were you on the bottom or top of the pile?
>
> How did this happen?
>
> Tell me exactly what you think is wrong with you.
>
> Do you think you need an operation? Why or why not?
>
> Were you able to help another injured letter? How?

From *Story Dramas,* published by Good Year Books. Copyright © 1997 Sarah Jossart & Gretchen Courtney.

After modeling the doctor/patient interview with some student letters, put students in pairs. Ask students to take turns enacting the scene between the injured letters and Dr. Letters.

TEACHER AS NARRATOR: What should the parents do to make sure the young letters don't climb the tree again? Should they be punished by being sent to their room, or should they have some chores assigned to them?

Students should make a list in their groups of all the possible ways to make sure that the young letters are safe. Suggest they share the list with the whole group.

Have students write a diary entry telling about their eventful day in the role of a letter: for example, climbing the tree, falling, going to the doctor, and being talked to by their parents.

Read aloud pages 27–30.

FOLLOW-UP ACTIVITIES

Ask students to

- Choose another letter and tell why they want to be that letter.
- Write the sequel to this story—what happens under the full moon?
- Write an accident report as if they are Dr. Letters.
- Write a letter to a friend warning him or her not to climb big trees and why.
- Share several alphabet books. Have them discuss how the books are the same and different.
- Draw a picture of their favorite letter. Suggest they add eyes, nose, and other features to give the letter a personality.

STORY DRAMA

"FIVE LITTLE DUCKS"

Based on the song from Raffi Songs to Read
by Raffi
(Five little ducks stray from their mother.)

This familiar tune and tale delights children from the very young to the not-so-young. But up until now, the disappearance of the five little ducks has not been so intriguing. This drama re-creates the time-honored tale with the students taking the roles of the disappearing ducks and creating a life for them outside and beyond the text.

A great benefit to using a familiar text is that students who are not proficient in English can still perform and enjoy this drama. The students then learn the words easily by associating them with words in their own language.

TEACHER AS MRS. DUCK *(showing cover of the book to students):* This is a picture of my family. I am Mrs. Duck, the red one. I have five lovely children swimming with me. My children and I LOVE to go on outings. Oh my, yes, we have such fun together. Why, just the other day, we swam all the way down to the bridge over the river to eat the bread crumbs that the children threw to us from the bridge. That was a grand day. Yes it was. Well, we almost lost Cynthia that day. Cynthia, Cynthia, are you in here, dear? *(Looks around the room expectantly, waiting for a student to respond. If a student responds, asks her or him the following questions.)*

> Would you please tell us about your adventure down at the bridge, when the dog jumped in the water after the bread?
>
> Were you scared, dear?
>
> Will you ever go down to the bridge again?

(If a student does not respond, goes on in the role of Mrs. Duck.)

Well, Cynthia must be out pruning her feathers. Let me tell you what happened. Cynthia was the one closest to the bridge, and she was eating the biggest pieces of bread. Before I could swim up close to her, a large black dog jumped into the water after an especially large chunk of bread. Poor Cynthia didn't look up quickly enough and the dog landed—splat—right on top of her. She went under, the dog went under, and there was great splashing and excitement. I dove under the water and pulled Cynthia out from under the dog, and the dog's owner jumped in to rescue the dog. We swam away from there as fast as we could paddle.

From Story Dramas, published by Good Year Books. Copyright © 1997 Sarah Jossart & Gretchen Courtney.

Ask students to choose one of the ducks from the cover and then stand up and pretend to be that duck. Try some waddling, quacking, and swimming.

Read aloud pages 1–5. (Pages are not numbered.)

TEACHER AS MRS. DUCK: Oh my! Oh dear. Oh no! One of my ducklings is missing! Where is the green duckling? Oh, where is the green duckling?

Students can discuss as a group where the green duckling might be. As a class, make a list of places where Mrs. Duck could look and a list of things she could do to find the lost duckling. Create a "Lost Duck" poster to hang up around the area.

Read aloud pages 6–24 to the class. As each consecutive duckling disappears, use a more distressed voice.

Have students draw a picture of where the ducklings went and what they did. Suggest they share their pictures with a small group of other students.

Read aloud pages 26–30.

TEACHER AS MRS. DUCK: Oh, my children! My precious children! I missed you so much. Where have you been? What have you been doing? *(Interviews the students as ducks concerning their whereabouts during the fall and winter. Asks the students the following questions.)*
> Where did you live while you were gone?
> What did you do to find food?
> Is this your family with you?
> Will you please introduce them to me?

FOLLOW-UP ACTIVITIES
Ask students to
- Plan a welcome-home party for all of the returning ducks and their families.
- Be a duckling and write a letter to Mrs. Duck to be sent during the duckling's time away.
- Sing the song "Five Little Ducks."
- Redo the drama, changing the animal featured from a duck to another animal, such as a bear, bird, or cat.

GENRE

FANTASY

Modern fantasy is very satisfying for young students' imaginations. Fantasy broadens and extends early readers' sense of story. Students love the humor, magic, wit, and nonsense these stories provide. Fantasy stories manipulate setting, character, and time to achieve the world of make-believe.

STORY DRAMA

"KOALA LOU"

Based on the book by Mem Fox
(A tale of never-ending parental love)

Mem Fox tells the tale of a first-born koala and her distress when she feels alone and unloved as her many brothers and sisters are born. Koala Lou makes a plan for winning back her mother's love, and finds out that her mother loved her all along. "Koala Lou, I do love you."

The universal theme of devoted parental love is an excellent choice to wind a drama around. This book excites the students to rally around Koala Lou and help her achieve her quest.

The setting is Australia, the event is the Bush Olympics, and all the animals are there. Knowledge of the types of animals native to Australia is helpful, but Pamela Lofts's realistic, entertaining illustrations offer the students many possibilities for creating their own animal characters.

To prepare for the drama experience, gather art supplies—colored construction paper, glue, feathers, markers, crayons, and so on.

Read aloud the first page, showing the students the illustration depicting Koala Lou. (The pages are not numbered.)

TEACHER AS ANTEATER: Oooh, itch, itch, itch. It is so hard to scratch my tummy when I get an itch. I am an echidna. Sometimes my friends call me a spiny anteater. I love to eat ants, especially the big, juicy ones. Another thing I love is playing soccer. I have to use my snout to hit the ball, but I am getting better at it. I also just love Koala Lou. She has been my best friend since I was five years old. She was on my soccer team last year. She is a really good goalie. You know, she has so many brothers and sisters though, that when I go to her house to play, sometimes I can't even find her!

Have each student pretend to be an animal that is native to Australia, such as a kangaroo, koala, parrot, crocodile, or an emu.

Read aloud page 2.

TEACHER AS NARRATOR: You all know Koala Lou, don't you? She lives over there in that tall gum tree behind the turn in the river *(pointing).* Tell me, how did you meet her? *(Continues to interview the students using the following questions.):*
    Does she play with you?
    Have you met her family? What did you think of them?
    What kind of animal are you?
    What is your name?
    Where do you live?
    Are you good at sports? Which ones?
    What do you and Koala Lou like to do together?

Ask students to turn to a neighbor and introduce themselves. Tell them to talk to each other about Koala Lou.

TEACHER AS ANTEATER: I love picnics. There are so many ants, ants, ants. Koala Lou and all the animals from the neighborhood are here today. There is so much food. I see the parrot family over by the ring toss, and who is that? It must be the emu and her little sister. I am going to play ball with them later this afternoon.

Have the children in their animal roles form small groups and talk about what they would do at the picnic. Then have them return to their seats and write a journal or diary entry retelling all the events that took place at the picnic.

Read aloud pages 3–9.

As a whole group, have students talk about the things Koala Lou could do to let her mother know the following: that she loves her, that she wants her mother to love her, that she wants her mother to say "I love you." Ask students to write Koala Lou letters telling her their best ideas to get her mother's love and attention.

Read aloud pages 10–12.

> **TEACHER AS NARRATOR:** Koala Lou has asked you to help her get ready for this big event, the Bush Olympics. What type of exercises and activities do you think will help her prepare the most for this event? *(Lists students' responses on the board and discusses what would make a well-balanced fitness program, and why.)*

Tell students that Koala Lou has asked them to help her train. Have them choose exercises and plan a fitness routine. Ask them to demonstrate the safe and proper way to perform all of these exercises.

Read aloud pages 13–17.

> **TEACHER AS NARRATOR:** The big day is finally here. As you know, in Australia, the sun can be very hot, so many of the animals here will wear hats to protect themselves from the sun. In fact, this is such a special occasion, they will probably wear their best hats. *(Discusses the illustration, focusing on the uniqueness of the hats.)*

Pretending they are animals, have students turn to the animal next to them and describe what the hat they will wear looks like. Then using paper, feathers, paints, and so on, create the hats. (If time does not permit the construction of hats, draw the hats on a piece of paper.)

Read aloud pages 18–21.

From *Story Dramas,* published by Good Year Books. Copyright © 1997 Sarah Jossart & Gretchen Courtney.

> **TEACHER AS NARRATOR:** Oh my, Koala Klaws has broken the record for the gum-tree climbing event. Do you think Koala Lou can do better? *(Polls the class, asking who the class thinks will win, and why.)*

Read aloud pages 22–30.

FOLLOW-UP ACTIVITIES

Ask students to

- Discuss why the kookaburra on the last page is so happy.
- Plan and record their own personal fitness programs.
- Write a note to their own mothers or caregivers, to tell them they love them. Add a picture.
- Find out more about the animals they created. Suggest they write a mini-report.
- Write a description of their hat to sell in a catalog.

STORY DRAMA

"FOURTH DAY: A DAY IN THE MARKETPLACE — UJAMMA"

Based on the story in It's Kwanzaa Time!
by Linda and Clay Goss
(A repetitive folk tale)

The seven principles of Kwanzaa are unity *(umoja)*, self-determination *(kujichagulia)*, collective work and responsibility *(ujima)*, cooperative economics *(ujamma)*, purpose *(nia)*, creativity *(kuumba)*, and faith *(imani)*. Kwanzaa, as the introduction in the book states, is a relatively new African American holiday. The word *Kwanzaa* is derived from the Swahili word meaning "first" or "first fruits of harvest." It is based on a rich melting of many ancient traditions, all of them promoting celebration and unity. The seven days of Kwanzaa are celebrated from December 26 through January 1. Similar to the Jewish and Christian celebrations in December, candles are symbolic and are lit for each of the seven days and the seven principles.

The story selected for this drama is "Fourth Day: A Day in the Marketplace—Ujamma." The classroom takes on the look of an open-air African marketplace while students practice the principle of cooperative economics. Students take on roles as marketplace vendors, selling anything from marbles to rugs to pigs. The story is written in the form of a repetitive folk tale, a story form familiar to young students. They will easily realize the pattern and repetition while following the Tortoise on his quest for sweet potato pie.

Read aloud the first paragraph of the story, beginning on page 32. Stop before Tortoise's song.

> **TEACHER AS MARKETPLACE VENDOR:** I come here each Saturday with my apples to sell. I grow all types of apples, from red to yellow to green. I load up my cart early in the morning and travel thirty-five miles from my home to sell as many apples as I can to the people who come to buy. *(Addresses class as if they are buyers at the marketplace.)* Apples, ripe and juicy, make pies, and cobblers, apples for sale.

Divide the students into small groups and have them discuss what they could sell at a marketplace. Once they have decided on their product, have them draw, on a large piece of paper, a picture of the front of their booth. Have them tape it to the front of their desks so that the room takes on the look of an African marketplace.

Students in groups discuss and prepare a short "sales pitch" for the crowd, similar to the apple vendor's. Once the students are prepared, have all the groups shout out the quality of their wares to the rest of the marketplace.

> **TEACHER AS BUYER** *(questioning students in their roles):*
> I have seen you here before. How often do you come?
> Why is your product better than someone else's in the marketplace?
> How do you produce your product?
> Are you willing to barter with people? Why or why not?
> Tell about the most interesting thing that has happened to you while you were selling your wares at the market.

Read aloud the rest of pages 32–33, all but the last line.

TEACHER AS VENDOR: All of you have seen the monkey drink the milk. What do you think should happen to the monkey? What should the tortoise do about this?

Have students form pairs and ask them to discuss the questions above and then share their answers with the whole group.

Record the students' responses. Ask the class to develop some suggestions, rules, or laws to control theft in the marketplace. List these on the board.

Read aloud last line of page 33 through page 37 until Tortoise takes the baskets.

TEACHER AS VENDOR: Here comes that tortoise now. Have you heard this story? Everyone he meets keeps stealing his wares. I just don't know what he is going to do. He has had so much trouble today. Oh, look! Here he comes, right by your booth.

Have students write down individually what they would say to Tortoise, what advice they would give him as he passes by their booth. Ask them to share their ideas with the rest of the vendors at their booth.

Read aloud from the bottom of page 37 through page 39.

FOLLOW-UP ACTIVITIES
Ask students to
- Write a list of all the foods they could make with sweet potatoes.
- Write a letter to Tortoise thanking him for the taste of sweet potato pie.
- Write an apology letter to Tortoise from the sweet potato man, fabric lady, honey gatherers, egg man, or the basket weaver.
- Write a story or a description of a time they have been to a marketplace, fair, or flea market.

STORY DRAMA
"WHO WANTS ARTHUR?"

Based on the book by Amanda Graham
(Ordinary things can be special.)

Arthur is an ordinary brown dog that wants a home. The other pets in the pet store are being sold, but no one selects Arthur, even when he tries so hard to be accepted. Arthur finally quits trying and discovers he is wanted. He finds a new home with Melanie and her grandpa.

The drama begins as you try to convince students to take home an ordinary brown dog named Arthur. Some students will take an ordinary brown dog named Arthur with no questions asked. Others will not accept an ordinary brown dog, no matter how hard you try to sell them on the idea.

A favorite part of the drama is when the students play the role of Arthur pretending to be other animals. Arthur first pretends to be a rabbit. Students are often hesitant at first, but a few may play the role of Arthur by wiggling their little noses, sticking out their teeth, and hopping around the room. When you ask for volunteers to show Arthur pretending to be a fish, hands may be up all over the room. You may even have to limit the sharing to "new" ideas only.

After the drama, show students the sequels, *Educating Arthur* and *Always Arthur*. Who would want an ordinary brown dog named Arthur? They may all want Arthur!

When Arthur got to his new house he played with the Melanie. They played cech and they ran together She didint care if he was a ordinary brown dog.

TEACHER AS WRITER: I am a writer from a well-known magazine, and I've been sent out to write an article about people and their pets. I've been sent to your area because I've been told you are looking for pets of your own. I understand each of you has been saving your money for a long time.

Ask for volunteers to introduce themselves and tell about the pet they want, what kind of pet it is, what it looks like, why they want that pet, and the name they might give the pet.

> **TEACHER AS WRITER** (*questioning students in their roles*):
>   Would you consider Arthur as a name for your pet? Why or why not?
>   What did they do to raise money to buy a pet?
>   Would you choose an ordinary dog for a pet? Why or why not?
> (*If a student doesn't have an idea for a pet, you might suggest an "ordinary" dog to talk about.*)

Read aloud pages 4–7. Ask for volunteers to demonstrate Arthur's practicing to be a rabbit.

Read aloud pages 8–13.

> **TEACHER AS WRITER:** Some of you purchased snakes today. I saw you coming out of the pet store, and I have some questions I would like to ask you.
>   Why did you select a snake?
>   What kind of snake did you select?
>   Can you describe your snake?
>   Why did you choose the snake over Arthur?
>   What will you do with your pet snake?
>   How do you care for a pet snake?
>   What tricks will you teach it?
>   How does your family feel about your new pet?
>   What will you name your pet snake?

Read aloud pages 14 and 15. Ask for volunteers to demonstrate Arthur practicing to be a fish.

Read aloud pages 16–23 and then ask students to pretend they are Arthur.

> **TEACHER AS WRITER** (*questioning students in the role of Arthur*):
>   How are you feeling?
>   Why do you think no one has chosen you?
>   Are you trying too hard or not hard enough? Explain.
>   What will you try next?
>   Will you give up? Why or why not?

Now ask student to pretend they are Mrs. Humber, the owner of the pet store.

> **TEACHER AS WRITER** *(questioning students in the role of Mrs. Humber):*
> How do you really feel about Arthur?
> What are you going to do now?
> Would you consider taking Arthur home with you? Why or why not?
> Would you consider giving him away?
> Have you ever had another pet in your store like Arthur? Explain.

Have students form small groups. Ask them what advice they have for Arthur. Have them come up with one idea that might solve his problem. Remember, all Arthur wants is a home with a pair of old slippers to chew. Ask what advice they have for Mrs. Humber. Have them come up with one idea that might help her sell Arthur or find a home for him. Ask the class to share ideas and make a list of ideas on the board. Discuss the possibilities.

Read aloud pages 24–27.

> **TEACHER** *(questioning students):*
> Does Melanie want Arthur? Why or why not?
> Will Grandpa let her have an "ordinary" dog like Arthur? Why or why not?
> Will Arthur want to go home with her? Why or why not?
> What questions do you think Arthur might ask Melanie if he could talk?

Read aloud pages 28–30.

FOLLOW-UP ACTIVITIES

Ask students to

- Write a group or individual sequel to the story, such as "Arthur and Melanie's Adventures," "Arthur's New Home," or "The Slippers and Arthur."
- Pretend they are the writer and write an article about people and their pets.
- Make a list of things they could teach Arthur to do.
- Write about or draw a picture of a pet they think would have a hard time finding a home.
- Draw a picture of their favorite pet and write or tell about it.
- Listen to or read published sequels, *Educating Arthur* and *Always Arthur,* by Amanda Graham.
- Ask their parents to bring in their family pet to share with the group.

From *Story Dramas*, published by Good Year Books. Copyright © 1997 Sarah Jossart & Gretchen Courtney.

STORY DRAMA
"DINOSAUR BOB"

Based on the book by William Joyce
(Explores tolerance and acceptance within a community.)

What a winning combination for young students—dinosaurs and baseball! When the adventurous Lazardo family finds a very large dinosaur on one of their trips, the excitement is just beginning. Dinosaur Bob is a reptile with a mind of his own, and the small community where the Lazardos live is not quite used to a dinosaur of its very own.

Imagine the problems when a dinosaur moves into town! Bob is a likable fellow, but as students create their own characters, each has a reason to either support or reject the towering creature. According to the students participating in this drama, Bob has some very bad habits.

Read aloud page 1. (Pages are not numbered.)

TEACHER AS NEIGHBOR: The Lazardos, yes, now that's an interesting family. I have lived next door to them for, let's see now, twenty years. Remember the time they brought home the Bengal tiger? That was the most excitement this town of Pimlico Hills had had in a long time. My, my, I haven't seen so many neighbors out of their houses since the Fourth of July fireworks. It seems like we are all waiting for the Lazardos to come home from their vacation to see what they will bring this time. *(Interviews the students, using the following questions.)*

Are you a neighbor of the Lazardos? Who are you and where do you live?

How long have you known the Lazardos, and how did you meet them?

What do you think they will bring home from their trip?

Are you taking care of the Lazardos' house or pets while they are away? Explain.

Why are the Lazardos an interesting family?

Read aloud pages 2–3.

Have students pretend they are Scotty, Zelda, and Velma and write a postcard to a friend or neighbor back in Pimlico Hills. Remind them to put a postcard-style picture on the front.

Read aloud pages 4–9.

TEACHER AS CAPTAIN BLOWHORN: I am Captain Blowhorn, and I am the captain of the luxury liner *Mayfair*. My crew and I have been preparing for weeks for a unique passenger named Bob. Bob has some special requirements. He is a dinosaur, and a rather large dinosaur too. Why, just the food preparation alone is unbelievable. *(Interviews students, using the following questions.)*

What type of crew member are you? What is your name?

What preparations have you been making for Bob's special trip?

What is the most difficult thing to get ready and why?

Have you seen Bob?

What did you think when you saw him?

What problems do you think you might have because Bob is on the luxury liner?

What have you heard the other passengers say about Bob?

Ask students to form small groups and write down a list of the food items the ship will need to keep Bob fed. Have them share these lists with the rest of the groups.

Read aloud pages 10–25. Then ask students to play the role of Bob.

TEACHER *(questioning students playing the role of Bob):*

Why do think you are in trouble?

Why did you enjoy the fingerprinting?

Do you want to go back to Africa? Why or why not?

What do you think you can do to change the mayor's mind?

What do you think the Lazardos can do to change the mayor's mind?

Ask students to pretend they are the neighbors again and write a letter to the mayor, telling him why Bob should or should not stay in Pimlico Hills.

Read aloud pages 26–31.

From *Story Dramas*, published by Good Year Books. Copyright © 1997 Sarah Jossart & Gretchen Courtney.

Students should get back in their small groups and discuss the following questions:

What do you think will happen when the Lazardos and Bob return home?

If you were the mayor, what would you do when they return?

Why do you think Bob chose Pimlico Hills instead of someplace else?

What do you think Bob will need to do so the town will accept him again?

Read aloud pages 32–41.

FOLLOW-UP ACTIVITIES

Ask students to

- Write additional lyrics to "The Ballad of Dinosaur Bob," found on pages 42–43.
- Write a paragraph describing why the town decides to let Bob stay.
- Describe the Lazardo family from Bob's point of view.
- Write about what they would do with a dinosaur living in their town.
- Write a list of things Bob should not do, so he stays out of trouble.
- Write a newspaper report about the opening baseball game.
- Draw a picture of Bob playing baseball.
- Read or listen to nonfiction dinosaur books. Tell the class what type of dinosaur you think Bob is.

STORY DRAMA

"FRITZI FOX FLEW IN FROM FLORIDA"

Based on the book by Leah Komaiko
(A story of friendship and house guests.)

Fritzi Fox flies in from Florida for her first visit to snow country. Fritzi Fox has some unusual habits as a house guest, and the hosting child is in for some surprises.

Have you entertained an unusual guest? If appropriate, share the story with your students. By sharing personal stories, we demonstrate to our students the elements of a story. These demonstrations help students develop their sense of story, a skill needed to be a reader and writer.

> **TEACHER AS FRIEND OF FRITZI FOX:** We are all at the _____ (inserts
> *school name*) Airport waiting for Fritzi Fox to arrive from Florida. We are friends
> and relatives of Fritzi Fox. We have a few minutes before her flight arrives, so let's
> get to know each other.

Students form pairs and introduce themselves to their partners. Have them tell
the partners their name and one thing they know about Fritzi Fox. (Suggestions
for things they might tell about Fritzi are hobbies, interests, habits, favorite
book, favorite sport, and favorite or least favorite food.) Have students volunteer
to introduce their partner, telling that person's name and the one thing they
learned about Fritzi.

> **TEACHER AS MS. TRAVEL:** I am Ms. Travel, the ticket agent here at _____
> Airport. I've enjoyed listening to all of you getting to know each other. I'm interest-
> ed in knowing more about you and about Fritzi Fox. *(Questions students in their
> roles.)*
> How long have you known Fritzi Fox?
> If you are a relative, how are you related to Fritzi Fox?
> Why is Fritzi Fox coming to visit?
> How long will Fritzi Fox be staying?
> Is anyone willing to take her home? Why or why not?
> How will you know Fritzi Fox when she gets off the plane? What will she be
>   wearing?
> What do you and Fritzi like to do together?

> **TEACHER AS ANNOUNCER:** Ladies and gentlemen, the plane from
> Florida has just arrived at Gate 101A. Please step aside and let the passengers
> through. The party meeting Fritzi Fox is requested to remain close to the
> gate to meet her as she arrives.

Read aloud pages 1–13. (Pages are not numbered.) Have students pretend
they are Fritzie's roommate.

> **TEACHER** *(questioning students in the role of the person sharing a room with Fritzi Fox):*
>
> What do you think of Fritzi Fox?
>
> Are you glad she came? Why or why not?
>
> Why do you think she came to visit?
>
> Are you glad she is sharing your room? Why or why not?
>
> Will you be able to sleep tonight? Why or why not?
>
> What do you think Fritzi Fox is doing with her suitcase?

Have students now pretend to be Fritzie Fox.

> **TEACHER** *(questioning students in the role of Fritzi Fox):*
>
> Are you glad you came? Why or why not?
>
> What do you think of the family you are staying with?
>
> Why are you so quiet?
>
> What friend or relative did you enjoy meeting at the airport? Why?
>
> Why can't you sleep?
>
> What are you doing with your suitcase?

Show the pictures on pages 14 and 15. Read aloud pages 16–27, showing pictures as you read the text.

> **TEACHER** *(questioning students in the role of the student who lives at the house where Fritzi is visiting):*
>
> What do you think of Fritzi Fox now?
>
> Are you glad she came? Why or why not?
>
> Are you glad you are sharing your room with her? Why or why not?
>
> Will you be able to sleep tonight? Why or why not?
>
> Have you ever had such an experience? If so, what?
>
> Will you invite Fritzi Fox to come stay another time? Why or why not?
>
> What was the best part of your experience with Fritzi Fox?

Read aloud page 28.

FOLLOW-UP ACTIVITIES

Ask students to

- Illustrate what Fritzi Fox had in her suitcase and write or tell about their night with her.
- Write a letter to Fritzi Fox thanking her for their evening together.
- Write or tell about another adventure Fritzi Fox could have in another suitcase.
- Write about their trip to Florida to visit Fritzi Fox.
- Write about one of their friends.
- Make a list of things they could do with Fritzi Fox if she visited their home.
- Draw a picture telling about a trip they have taken with their family.

STORY DRAMA

"WILL'S MAMMOTH"

Based on the book by Rafe Martin
(An adventure about a boy with an active imagination)

Will believes there are woolly mammoths, so much so that this semi-wordless picture book takes us on an exciting woolly mammoth ride. Will rides his gigantic mammoth through a saber-toothed tiger attack, alongside the woolly rhinoceros, and by cave people from the past. At the end of the day, Will honestly reports that he rode his mammoth all day.

Students become the siblings of the imaginative, creative Will. They don't really know what to make of his behavior, so they decide to follow along on his outing. The familiar role of a sibling is enhanced by having a brother who believes in and plays with woolly mammoths.

Read aloud pages 1–5. (Pages are not numbered.)

From *Story Dramas*, published by Good Year Books. Copyright © 1997 Sarah Jossart & Gretchen Courtney.

TEACHER AS PETE: My name is Pete, and Will is my brother. I really like him, but he is such a mess! His room is a mess, his clothes are a mess, everything he does is a mess! I am two years older than Will, so I know that there aren't any woolly mammoths still living. Will, he really believes that these creatures are still around. I am really worried about him. The kids at school are starting to talk about him. I mean, really, woolly mammoths?! Will is your brother, also. We are all in the same big happy family. *(Interviews students, using the following questions.)*

> What is your name and how old are you?
>
> What do you think of your brother?
>
> Do you two get along or do you fight?
>
> Do you have to share a room with Will? If yes, what is that like? If no, what does your room look like?
>
> Do you think there are really woolly mammoths alive today? Why or why not?

Will has been acting really funny today. No, I mean really funny. I think I am going to follow him today. It looks like he is going outside to play. I get the feeling something strange is going on. Come on! You come too! Just make sure that Will doesn't see us.

Read aloud pages 6–9.

TEACHER AS NARRATOR *(asking the students the following questions)*:

> Where did these animals come from?
>
> Are they really woolly mammoths? How do you know?
>
> Is this safe? Why or why not?
>
> Is Will going to be okay? Explain why you think so.
>
> Where are these animals going?
>
> What do you think is going to happen next?

Read aloud pages 10–11.

TEACHER AS PETE: I can't believe my eyes. I think I have just seen a woolly mammoth. I am worried about Will. Let's keep following him! *(Pause.)* Look ahead, there is trouble! We can't let that baby mammoth fall into the crevice.

Have students form small groups and then discuss ways to work together to save the baby mammoth. Ask them to share their ideas with the rest of the group.

Read aloud pages 12–19.

> **TEACHER AS PETE:** I am so cold. It is freezing outside today. Look, over there is a fire and CAVE PEOPLE! Are those really cave people?

> **TEACHER AS NARRATOR** *(questioning students):*
> What will you say to these people?
> Will they understand you? Why or why not?
> How will you communicate?
> Will they be friendly? Why or why not?
> Will they share their food with you? What will they be eating?

Read aloud pages 20–25.

> **TEACHER AS PETE:** Whoa. That's Mom calling. What are we going to tell her?

In their small groups as Will's siblings, have students decide what they are going to tell their mothers when they get home. Have them share this with the rest of the class and decide which explanation is the best.

Read aloud pages 26–30.

FOLLOW-UP ACTIVITIES

Ask students to
- Write or draw a picture of their adventures today.
- Form pairs and hold a conversation between their character and Will.
- Form pairs and hold a conversation between their character and Will's mother.
- Write or draw a picture of what it would be like to ride on a mammoth.

From *Story Dramas*, published by Good Year Books. Copyright © 1997 Sarah Jossart & Gretchen Courtney.

STORY DRAMA

"THE REINDEER CHRISTMAS"

Based on the book by Moe Price
(Explains the magical sleigh and its flying reindeer.)

One Christmas, before the days of the reindeer-pulled sleigh, Santa finds himself ready to retire when he can no longer deliver all of the presents by foot. This book explains one of the Christmas myths. Elwin, with the help of the elf community, creates the red and gilt sleigh only to have trouble finding someone qualified to pull it.

This drama is an excellent accompaniment to the poem drama, "A Visit from St. Nicholas," on pages 35–39. Creating this drama as a prelude to Santa's visit sets the stage for the students' conversation with the miniature reindeer and Merry Holiday on top of the Noel house.

Read aloud pages 1–4. (Pages are not numbered.)

TEACHER AS ELWIN: I am Elwin, Santa's chief elf. I have a very responsible job, and I am very proud of it. I worked very hard to earn the job of chief elf. I started out in the mail room answering all of the children's wish letters. Next, I worked in the kitchen with Mrs. Claus, making all the Christmas goodies. After that, I was transferred to the doll-painting room. I really liked that job. The people were very nice and friendly. It has been ten years since I started with Santa, and my whole family works here. My mother is in charge of all the stuffed toys, and my father runs the train department. My brothers and sisters are all in various departments around the North Pole.

Read aloud pages 5–6.

TEACHER AS NARRATOR (*showing students the illustration*): Find yourself on this page. Which elf are you? What is your name? (*Continues to question a few students using the following questions.*)

Why are you off work today?

Which department of Santa's workshop do you work in?

What specialty do you have?

Do you like your work? Why or why not?

How did you become one of Santa's helpers?

Does your family work here also? What do they do?

How long have you been working here?

Have students pretend they are elves. Tell them they have a day off from the workshop, to enjoy the winter weather. They do not often get to see elves from other departments. In pairs, they should interview each other to find out all about the other elf.

Then have students tell the class about the elf that he or she interviewed.

Read aloud pages 7–8.

Have students form small groups and then discuss and draw a design for a sleigh. Ask them to share their design with the rest of the class. Vote on the best design.

Read aloud pages 9–14.

Have students design and create a poster advertisement for someone to pull Santa's sleigh. Put the posters up around the room.

Read aloud pages 15–22.

TEACHER AS NARRATOR: Santa is so worried. There doesn't seem to be an animal who has the ability to pull this magical sleigh. Wait, wait a minute. Is that someone coming up the drive, wanting to try out for the job?

Ask students to name an animal who could pull the sleigh. Have them pretend they are this animal and tell the rest of the group why they are the most qualified for this job.

Read aloud pages 23–30.

FOLLOW-UP ACTIVITIES

Ask students to

- Look at the illustration on page 31 and write or tell a story about this child and what Santa is doing in his or her room.
- Get in their small groups and write an advertisement selling their sleigh, which was not selected by Elwin and the elf community.
- Retell the story, having one of the other animals pulling the sleigh on Christmas Eve.
- Write a job description for Elwin and a want-ad for someone to fill this position if Elwin retired today.
- Write a letter to Santa, asking him any questions they might have.
- Tell another person about what it would be like to ride in Santa's sleigh.

STORY DRAMA

"WHISTLING DIXIE"

Based on the book by Marcia Vaughan
(Unusual creatures visit Dixie's house.)

This drama is especially fun to perform close to the Halloween season. It works well at any time, but during the time of creatures and ghosts and monsters, Dixie's encounters with the churn turners, bogeyman, and the mist sisters are especially realistic. This drama is set in Hokey Pokey Swamp, which stretches the imagination of the students. The colorful language used by Dixie's family begins to creep into the vocabulary of the student-created characters, making them more believable and enjoyable to enact. This drama has an unusual twist. The entire book is read aloud first, and then the students go back into the text to create characters, solve problems, and become a part of the story.

Read aloud the entire text, showing students all of the illustrations and stopping to discuss or react as the story progresses. Create this drama in a bus-stop setting, waiting for the bus to pick up students from school in Hokey Pokey Swamp on a Friday afternoon.

TEACHER AS SARAH: I am so excited and a little bit scared. My very best friend, Dixie Lee, asked me over to her house for a slumber party tonight. I really want to go because lots of other people are going to be there too, but sometimes Dixie Lee's house has UNUSUAL THINGS going on there. You know, even though Dixie Lee and I are both eight years old, she is so much braver than I am. Why, she is always saying, "Sarah, you are as scaredy as a creeper frog in a fish pond." *(Directs questions to student group.)* Say, aren't you all going to the slumber party too? Dixie Lee told me she had invited all sorts of folks. I am new to Hokey Pokey Swamp and I don't know all of you yet. Tell me your names and how old you are. *(Calls on students quickly, like a roll call, having them select a name and an age between 3 and 20 that they would like to be.)* The bus is coming, I can hear the black crows flying off the pavement now. We better get lined up for the bus.

Have students divide into groups by their pretend age: ages 3–7 in one group, ages 8–12 in another group, and ages 13–20 in another group. While students are moving to their groups, push their desks or chairs into two rows with two seats in each row, resembling the seating on a bus.

TEACHER AS SARAH *(turning to a student in your group to model this discussion):* Hi, I have seen you at lunch time. My name is Sarah Louanne Peters. What is your name? Are you going to Dixie Lee's house? Are you scared? Did you hear that there are creatures that come at night to Dixie's house? I might ask my cousin Bill to come with me. He is the best wrestler in the whole county. Why, he has more trophies than a porcupine has quills. Are you going to take someone with you? Why are you taking that person?

Have students talk to the others in their bus group and find out if they are going to Dixie Lee's house and whether they are scared. Dixie Lee said they could bring someone with them. Whom will they bring?

TEACHER AS NARRATOR: Here comes the bus. Get on the bus everyone and find your seats. Remember, younger children in front, older children in the back. *(Students sit in the seats arranged like a bus or on the floor in a similar fashion.)*

From *Story Dramas*, published by Good Year Books. Copyright © 1997 Sarah Jossart & Gretchen Courtney.

> **TEACHER AS SARAH** (*putting a real or imagined backpack or school bag on her lap*): I am going to take my bag to Dixie Lee's. I have been there before, and all they had to eat was cattail stew! I am putting a sandwich and maybe some cookies in my bag so I don't have to eat cattails. They stick in your throat and make it hard to swallow. Why, last time I tried a bite of tickly-tail stew at Dixie Lee's house, I coughed so hard my shoes came untied. I'm going to make a list of all of the things I am going to take to Dixie Lee's house tonight. I will probably need a flashlight for walking around at night and I certainly need my good-luck laser ring I got at the county fair last summer. . . .

Have students make a list of all the things they will want to take with them in their pretend bags when they go to Dixie Lee's house.

> **TEACHER AS SARAH:** Oh, here is my stop! I will see you all at Dixie Lee's house tonight.

> **TEACHER AS NARRATOR:** Hokey Pokey Swamp is a long way from the hard road. You have to walk along a vine-covered trail to get to Dixie Lee's house, but finally you arrive.

Turn out some or all of the lights in the room. Divide the class into groups of four or five students. Tell students to imagine Hokey Pokey Swamp all around them. Instruct them to look at their feet sinking into the mud and listen for the cattails moving and the frogs jumping down by the water. Have them reach out and try to touch the cool, wet grass and the prickly bushes and weeping willow branches all around them.

Gather students in small groups and have them select an animal that they might have found in Hokey Pokey Swamp. Then create a creature, ghost, or monster that will come to the house that night. In their groups, they should decide how the animal they have selected will ward off the creature, ghost, or monster. Have one student act as narrator, while the other students pantomime the scene where the creature, ghost, or monster meets the animal and is frightened off.

Share all of the groups' pantomimes.

FOLLOW-UP ACTIVITIES

Ask students to

- Create a picture of the scene they have just enacted between the creature, ghost, or monster and their animal. Write about their picture with a classmate.
- Take the role of Dixie Lee and write a journal entry, diary entry, or letter to their grandmother describing the night of the party.
- Draw a picture of the most unusual animal creature they have ever seen.

STORY DRAMA

"KING BIDGOOD'S IN THE BATHTUB"

Based on the book by Audrey Wood
(A silly story that involves problem-solving)

This silly story tickles the minds of young students. They enjoy predicting how to get the king out of the tub and rejoice in the solution of a child and the silliness of the adults.

This drama works well in kindergarten and first grade. Second- and third-graders can get stuck on the inappropriate behavior of having others in the king's tub. Be prepared for this reaction and gently remind the students that this story and drama call for some silliness and pretending.

Drama preparation: Copy the ball invitation below, roll it up as a scroll, and tie it with a ribbon.

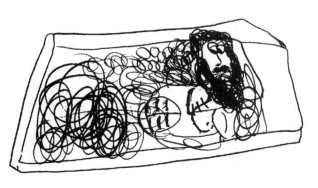

**The People Of
King Bidgood's Kingdom
Are Invited To
A Masquerade Ball
On (current date)
To Be Held in the Bathtub
In King Bidgood's Castle
All Loyal Country Men
and
Women Are Invited.
Costumes Are Required.**

From *Story Dramas*, published by Good Year Books. Copyright © 1997 Sarah Jossart & Gretchen Courtney.

TEACHER AS LADY BEE: Welcome to the kingdom of King Bidgood. We are all fellow countrymen and countrywomen of this kingdom. My name is Lady Bee. I am the recorder of the king's court. I keep track of what is happening in the kingdom. Since we live in so many places in this kingdom, it is important we get to know each other.

Students form pairs and then introduce themselves to each other, telling their names as well as their positions in the kingdom. Have volunteers introduce the people they have met.

As roles are introduced to the group, question each character in his or her role. For example:

TEACHER AS LADY BEE *(to Knight):*

    What was your toughest battle?

    How do you prepare for battle?

    What do you do when you are not in battle?

TEACHER AS LADY BEE *(to Cook):*

    What is the King's favorite dish?

    What foods does the King not like?

TEACHER AS LADY BEE *(to Prince):*

    Are you looking forward to being king?

    Why or why not?

TEACHER AS LADY BEE *(to Princess):*

    What is it like living in the castle?

    Where is your favorite place to play?

> **TEACHER AS LADY BEE:** Countrymen and countrywomen, we have a problem. I have just received word from the castle of King Bidgood that the king has been in the bathtub for hours and will not get out! We have been asked to gather some suggestions to take to the castle to help in this urgent matter.

Ask characters in their roles for suggestions. For example, ask what might the cook, knight, prince, and jouster do to help get the king out of the tub. List ideas and vote on the top three suggestions to take to the castle.

Read the text aloud to students starting at the first page of the story through the page where the king announces the dance. Then read the invitation to the ball. Take your time unrolling the scroll; the students' anticipation is worth these few extra seconds.

> **TEACHER** (*questioning characters about their experiences at the ball*):
> Are you enjoying the ball? Why or why not?
> Who do you think is wearing that fish costume? (*Shows the picture of the ball and locates the fish costume.*)
> How would you describe your costume for the masquerade ball?
> What is the most unusual costume you've seen?
> How has this dance been different from others you've attended?
> Did you have a conversation with the king? What did you talk about?
> What do you think about your king?
> What happened when the three suggestions were tried?

Read aloud the last three pages of the text.

FOLLOW-UP ACTIVITIES

Ask students to

- Write a journal entry from the viewpoint of the page, a character played in the drama, or the king.
- Draw an illustration of a costume worn to the ball and describe it in writing or tell about it during a sharing time.
- Write a newspaper article about the king's day in the tub. This article would be in the form of a who, what, when, where, why, and how report.
- Write a group or individual letter to the king from a character played in the drama. Include the character's suggestion for getting the king out of the tub.
- Write a daily schedule for the king or character played in the drama.

From *Story Dramas*, published by Good Year Books. Copyright © 1997 Sarah Jossart & Gretchen Courtney.

STORY DRAMA

"HEY, AL"

Based on the book by Arthur Yorinks
(A fantasy story with a moral)

All elementary students love the tale of Al and his faithful dog, Eddie, but second- and third-graders are especially taken with it. In this tale, a janitor named Al and his dog, Eddie, are persuaded by a large bird to give up their dull lives and come with him to paradise. Al and Eddie undertake this adventure only to find out they would be better off back in their one-room apartment.

This story drama takes on a festive or circus-type air with a few extras. All dramas can be done on the spur of the moment, but adding costuming and a few props adds variety. Name tags are a good idea. You may need two or three for each student, depending on how many characters are created. An assortment of hats and a feathered mask are fun, if possible. Martha, Al's neighbor, can wear a nurse's cap. Al can sport a baseball cap and carry a few tools in his pockets. A feathered mask works nicely for the large, mysterious bird. A stethoscope or white coat works well for the doctor.

During this drama, you might be surprised at the argumentative strategies employed by such young minds. This is demonstrated in the conversation between Al and Eddie when deciding whether or not they will go off with the large bird that has appeared in their bathroom. Once the students realize that saying, "Yes, you will," or "No, you won't," gets them nowhere, they employ various tactics to convince the other. The whole exchange can be very enlightening for the teacher.

Read aloud the first page of the story to the class. (Pages are not numbered.)

> **TEACHER AS MARTHA GOODWILL:** Hello. My name is Martha Goodwill, and I have just moved into your apartment building. I am so anxious to meet all of you, my new neighbors. I have just moved to this city and I am hoping we can be friends. I am a nurse and work the night shift at the hospital. I live alone except for my pet parakeet, Sam. Tell me about yourselves. *(Conducts short interview with a few students.)*
>
> What is your name?
>
> How long have you lived in this building?
>
> What job do you have?
>
> Do you live alone?
>
> Do you know Al, the janitor who lives downstairs?
>
> I noticed he has a dog. I am afraid of dogs. Tell me, is this dog friendly?

Have students form pairs. Then ask them to pretend they are apartment dwellers, and then interview their partners and introduce them to the rest of the neighbors.

> **TEACHER AS MARTHA GOODWILL:** Well, here we are at this apartment-tenants' meeting. I have heard that the landlord wants to raise our rents. I don't know about you, but I can't afford that right now. What do the rest of you think?

Have students discuss the pros and cons of a rent increase, taking the role of their newly created characters.

Read aloud pages 2 through the top of page 5, stopping before Al and Eddie make their decision.

Ask students to form pairs and have one student take the role of Al and the other take the role of Eddie. Role-play a discussion between Al and Eddie considering whether or not they should go with the bird. Have volunteers share their arguments.

Read aloud the bottom of page 5 through page 13.

Show the birds in this picture to the students. Have each choose a bird that he or she likes. Look at the type of legs each bird has, its beak, feathers, size, and other features. Ask them what calls their birds might make and how they might walk. Ask students to walk around the room as their birds in a "bird parade."

From *Story Dramas*, published by Good Year Books. Copyright © 1997 Sarah Jossart & Gretchen Courtney.

Read aloud pages 14 and 15.

> **TEACHER AS MARTHA GOODWILL:** Oh my, what day is it? Is it _____?
> Al always has dinner with his mom on _____days. She doesn't know where he
> is. She will be very worried. We have to do something. *(Passes out postcard-sized
> pieces of paper to use for writing.)*

Have students create a postcard from Al or Eddie to Al's mom. They can write
a message to Al's mother on one side of the card explaining what has happened.
On the other side, they can draw a picture of where they are.

Read aloud pages 16–19.

Have students beg to be rescued by writing a note and putting it in a bottle with
the hopes someone will find it.

> **TEACHER AS DR. MEDICINE:** Hello, I am Dr. Horatio Medicine. What seems
> to be the problem today? *(Interviews students role-playing the parts of Al and Eddie,
> who are turning into birds.)* Where does it hurt? When did these symptoms begin?
> Can you think of anything unusual you have done lately that might have caused
> this? Describe all of your symptoms.

Read aloud pages 20–23. Ask the students playing Al what they will do, now
that Eddie is missing. How will life be different? Have the other students offer
advice.

Read aloud the last two pages of text. Discuss what the ending means. Refer
back to the page that says, "But, ripe fruit soon spoils." Discuss what this means
and how it relates to the ending of the story.

FOLLOW-UP ACTIVITIES
Ask students to
- Draw a picture of what Al and Eddie's apartment looks like after they return
  home.
- Create a drawing of what they would look like if they turned into birds.
- Role-play a conversation between Al and his mother after he returns home.
- Shuffle the notes, distribute them to the class, and have the students write a
  response to the pleas for help.

GENRE

FICTION

Modern fiction has changed the genre of fiction for young children. Realistic stories relating to the elderly, cultural differences, the disabled, and differing family structures are abundant. Realistic fiction consists of stories where everything included could happen and is true to life experiences. When students read and listen to these stories, they gain insights into social relationships, their own identity, and their self-worth, as well as learn approaches to solving problems they are likely to encounter in our ever-changing society.

STORY DRAMA

"OLD HENRY"

Based on the book by Joan W. Blos
(Shows us how to live with all types of neighbors.)

Old Henry moves into a neighborhood and is quite content to be by himself and live with his bird and books. The neighbors, however, feel he is upsetting the neighborhood by the careless upkeep of his lawn and home. Pressures by the neighbors to change Old Henry finally take their toll and Old Henry leaves, but soon the neighborhood just doesn't seem the same without Old Henry. Old Henry discovers he misses the neighborhood too. Old Henry writes the mayor and asks if he may come back.

An old shirt and cap quickly turn you into the character of Old Henry. Take a little time as you adorn yourself with these props in front of your class to heighten the students' anticipation.

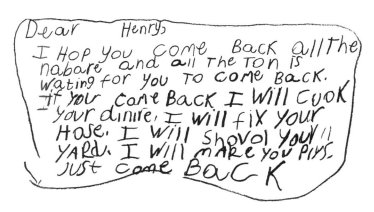

From *Story Dramas*, published by Good Year Books. Copyright © 1997 Sarah Jossart & Gretchen Courtney.

This story has all the characteristics of a good drama, but the most exciting part is solving the problem of a neighbor who does not seem to fit into the neighborhood. As students strive to solve the problem of the undesirable neighbor, new problems seem to appear. Here is a point that needs emphasizing: It is important to try to solve problems without creating new problems. As ideas are shared, the students evaluate the pros and cons of each idea before coming to a group consensus of how the situation should be handled. When the students are given the chance to play the role of the town mayor and write to Old Henry, some might apologize for the town's behavior and invite him back. Others might not invite Old Henry to return. After sharing the letters written by the students in the role of the mayor, students discover they have written a new ending to the story.

To prepare for the drama, create a sign with the wording, "Gone to Dakota." When ready to begin, read the book title to the class and show the picture on the cover of Old Henry.

> **TEACHER** (questioning the students):
> Who might Old Henry be?
> How do you think he got his name?
> Where do you think he came from?
> What do you think he likes to do?
> What do you think he might do in this story?
> To whom might the bird belong?
> Would you like to meet Old Henry? Why or why not?

Read aloud the first page. (Pages are not numbered.)

Play the role of the stranger, Old Henry, who has just arrived in a new neighborhood and wants to meet the neighbors.

> **TEACHER AS OLD HENRY:** Hello, neighbors. I am Old Henry, I've just moved into your neighborhood. I would like to meet you, my new neighbors. *(As the students watch, draws a simple house on the chalkboard and adds a tree, a broken-down fence, and some tall grass.)*

Students will play the role of the neighbors in the neighborhood. Encourage the students to "pretend" and introduce themselves to you, the new neighbor.

> **TEACHER AS OLD HENRY** *(questioning the students as neighbors):*
>   What can you tell me about my house?
>   Who used to live there?
>   Why did they move?
>   What can you tell me about this neighborhood?
>   Can you tell me about some of the people I might meet?

Encourage the students to ask "the stranger" some questions (where he came from, what he does, what he likes and dislikes, etc.).

> **TEACHER AS OLD HENRY:** I can't wait to be a part of this neighborhood. Thank you for giving me such a nice welcome. I've enjoyed meeting _____ *(names a few neighbors)* and learning about my new neighborhood.

Read aloud pages 2–8.

Students continue in the roles of the neighbors and you, the teacher, become a reporter (if you are wearing a costume for Old Henry don't forget to take it off).

> **TEACHER AS REPORTER:** I am a reporter for the _____ Press *(inserts local newspaper name).* I've been sent to find out what is happening in your neighborhood. I understand there has been a disturbance. Tell me about your problem. *(Encourages several neighbors to tell their views.)*
>   What do you think the neighborhood should do?
>   What would you suggest?
>   How can you get Henry to notice his place?
>   What could you do to help him?
>   Do you think he wants your help? Why or why not?

Read aloud pages 9 and 10.

Have students form groups of three: Each group should form a committee and come up with three ideas to get Henry interested in fixing up his place. Have them share their ideas with the whole group.

Read aloud pages 11–15.

From *Story Dramas*, published by Good Year Books. Copyright © 1997 Sarah Jossart & Gretchen Courtney.

> **TEACHER AS REPORTER** *(questioning students in their neighbor roles):*
> What are some things we could do to be nice?
> *(Brainstorms with neighbors some ideas and lists them on the board.)*
> Will these ideas work? Why or why not?
> Would you try them the second time, as the mayor says? Why or why not?
> Which idea is the very best? Why?

Read aloud pages 16–22 and tape the sign "Gone to Dakota" over the house drawn earlier on the chalkboard.

> **TEACHER AS REPORTER** *(talking to neighbors):*
> What has happened in your neighborhood since I last reported about a disturbance?
> How do you feel now about the situation?
> What will you do with the vacant house?
> Will you help take care of his property? Why or why not?
> Do you miss Henry? Why or why not?
> What do you know about Old Henry's disappearance?

Read aloud pages 23–26.

> **TEACHER AS REPORTER** *(questioning neighbors):*
> What should you neighbors do?
> How can you get Henry back?
> Will he come back? Why or why not?

Read aloud pages 27–29.

> **TEACHER AS REPORTER** *(questioning continues):*
> Will the mayor answer? Why or why not?
> Would you answer if you were the mayor?
> What would your answer be?

Have students pretend they are the mayor and write their answers to Henry. To make this more fun, make up a letterhead for the office of Mayor _____ (insert name of your mayor) and use the school's address for the return address. This activity can also be done as a group dictated letter. After several minutes of writing, ask for volunteers to submit their finished letters for reading aloud. Put on the old cap and become Old Henry once again. Read several letters to the class.

Show the students the last page of the book and talk about how they have actually written another ending to the story by writing their letters.

FOLLOW-UP ACTIVITIES
Ask students to
- Plan a welcome-back celebration.
- Design a welcome-back sign. Share the signs and display them around the room along with the book.
- Plan a welcome-back cheer for Old Henry. Share the cheers.
- Plan activities that involve being a good neighbor. Some possibilities are picking up trash, caroling, hanging May baskets, and so on. (On the first day of May, the tradition is to hang a basket of flowers on a door, ring the bell, and run away, letting the recipient guess who hung the flowers there.)
- Plan with your parents a time to do a neighborly deed. Think about going to visit senior citizens, helping out in a neighbor's yard, and so forth.
- Plan with your teacher a time the class could help greet parents at a school function.

STORY DRAMA
"THE MOON CAME TOO"

Based on the book by Nancy White Carlstrom
(A story written in verse from a child's point of view.)

A little girl packs her belongings to go to Grandma's house. She has many things she wants to take along, and this causes her mother some concern. Mother seems to think only the moon will be left behind. To the delight of the little girl and the reader, they discover after a long trip to Grandma's house that the moon does come too.

From *Story Dramas*, published by Good Year Books. Copyright © 1997 Sarah Jossart & Gretchen Courtney.

Even with no costumes, no stage directions, and no memorization, the presentation is dramatic. Each drama participant packs his or her bag to visit Grandma or some other special person. When limited to three items to take along, the decisions of what to take are as varied as the individuals in any group. To make it more interesting, each small group should come to a consensus as to what these three items will be. As part of the drama, students also play car games and sing.

Upon reading the ending of the book, students discover the moon is at Grandma's house too. This discovery alone makes this story worth sharing with your students.

> **TEACHER AS NARRATOR:** Each of you has a special person in your life, be it a cousin, friend, grandmother, grandfather, an aunt, or uncle. Tell us who this person is and a little about why this person is special to you. *(Lets students volunteer to tell about a special person.)* Pretend you have just decided to visit your special person. What expression do you have on your face?

Have students act out their expressions.

> **TEACHER AS NARRATOR:** We need to think about the things we would like to take with us when we visit our special people. Tell me what you would take with you, and why you are taking that item. *(Lets students share and lists all the ideas on the board.)* Each of you should think about your journey to your special person's home as you listen to the story of a child traveling to her grandma's house.

Read aloud pages 1–17. (Pages are not numbered.)

Have students form small groups.

> **TEACHER AS NARRATOR:** Mother has just told you that there is room in the car for only three items of your choice. With your group, look at the items listed on the board and select three things you will take. Your group must agree on the three items. Discuss in your group why these items would be the best to choose.

Have students discuss their selections. Then ask each group to share their decision and tell why each item was selected. Tally items on the board.

Read aloud pages 18–19.

Ask students to discuss what they like to do on a long drive, games they might play, what songs they might sing, and so on. If possible, do some of the ideas suggested; if not, select one or more of the following activities to do.

Sing "Old McDonald Had a Farm" or "Row, Row, Row Your Boat."

Play "I Spy" (describe something in the room and have the others guess what it is from the description).

Read aloud pages 20–23.

> **TEACHER AS NARRATOR** *(using the list of items checked, asks students to answer these questions):*
> What would be the first thing you would show your special person, and why?
> If you could exchange one of the three items for another item, what would you choose? Why?

> **TEACHER AS NEXT-DOOR NEIGHBOR:** I am your next-door neighbor, and I watched you pack all your things to go to your special person's house. I heard your mother say you could take only three things, but I also saw each of you sneak one small item into your pocket. Tell us what is in your pocket, why you wanted it along, and what you will do with it.

Have students think of what that item might be and share a description of it with the class.

Read aloud pages 24 through the end.

From *Story Dramas,* published by Good Year Books. Copyright © 1997 Sarah Jossart & Gretchen Courtney.

FOLLOW-UP ACTIVITIES

Ask students to

- Write a sequel to the story, telling all about the girl's visit to Grandma's.
- Draw and write about a special person.
- Write about a real visit to their grandma's house.
- Write a letter to a special person, thanking her or him for a real or pretend visit.
- Write a letter to a grandparent and mail it to them.
- Draw a picture of the item they put in their pocket and label it.
- Listen to or read *The Moon Is Following Me,* by Philip Heckman, and compare and contrast it with this story. (You might use a Venn diagram to illustrate this comparison.)
- Listen to or read *Follow the Moon,* by Sarah Weeks, a delightful story of a baby sea turtle following the moon. Compare it to *The Moon Came Too.*

STORY DRAMA

"AMAZING GRACE"

Based on the book by Mary Hoffman
(A lesson in perseverance)

Today's students are familiar with student actors, but they know little about the hard work that goes into getting those roles. This drama introduces the students to the audition and the perseverance it takes to be selected.

Amazing Grace loves to act out stories. She loves the roles of famous heroes and animals. Suddenly, when Grace is faced with a role others feel she cannot achieve, she does not give up.

To prepare for the drama presentation, copy the audition parts at the end of the drama. These parts are provided for your convenience, but it is more fun to use some of your class's favorite stories and characters. You will need to prepare these lines, or you might assign students the task of preparing lines for some of the class's favorite characters as part of a lesson on characterization. Another variation might be to have each student write his or her own character part from a favorite story or poem.

I like to be a president of the United States of America. My mom will vote for me to be president.

> **TEACHER AS HEAD OF STUDIO:** We are here at the Performing Arts Studio of _____ *(inserts your school's name).* Why, look over there. *(Directs attention to another area.)* I think I see _____ *(male or female actor).* What makes him/her such a good actor? You are also some of the best actors from all over the world. A series of plays will be given soon, and each of us is here to audition for a part in one of those plays. You will want to show the directors how well you can speak and act your parts.

Ask for volunteers to introduce themselves. Ask the students to tell the group their names, where they are from, and why they think they are among the best performers in the world.

> **TEACHER AS HEAD OF STUDIO** *(questioning students further in their roles):*
>   Who got you started in acting?
>   What roles have you played?
>   Is acting hard work? Why or why not?
>   How did you hear about these auditions?
>   What is the most fun about acting?
>   What acting part would you like?
>   If you could be like some other performer, who would it be? Why?
>   Do you expect to make money as an actor? Why or why not?

Read aloud the first page of text. (Pages are unnumbered and references will be made only to pages with text.)

> **TEACHER AS HEAD OF STUDIO** *(questioning students):*
>   What part would you want to play in the story of Cinderella? Why?
>   What part would you want to play in the story of The Three Little Pigs? Why?

Name several more stories your class has read, asking each time what role they would like to play and why they would select that role.

Read aloud text pages 2–12.

> **TEACHER AS HEAD OF STUDIO:** We will be holding auditions for Peter Pan as well as other roles *(or insert any other character you or your students have prepared)*. Each of you can decide what part you wish to audition for. You will be given a part your character would say in a play. Each of you can practice your part; think about how you will use your voice, move your body, and perform other actions you might use to best perform your character. You do not need to memorize your parts word for word.

Each student should decide which character he or she wants to audition for. See audition lines for Peter Pan, Cinderella, Wolf (from *The Three Little Pigs*), Chicken Little, Little Old Woman, and Humpty Dumpty. Lines from other stories prepared by you or the students may be used here instead of the prepared lines.

Model your script lines. Show action, feelings, and the use of voice.

Pass out parts and set a time limit for the "practice session." Students who show no interest in a part and cannot be encouraged to participate should meet with the teacher to plan their role as directors.

Teacher and "directors" should plan what they will look for in the auditions (loud voice, clear words, interesting actions, feeling, etc.). Make a list together. Have the directors give one positive comment for each audition. (Depending upon the size of your group, these comments might be rotated between the directors, allowing one comment for each audition.)

Read aloud text page 13 through the first paragraph of text page 19.

Each student performs his or her selected part. Directors then respond to the auditions in turn.

Read aloud the text starting with the second paragraph on page 19 through the end of the book.

From *Story Dramas*, published by Good Year Books. Copyright © 1997 Sarah Jossart & Gretchen Courtney.

FOLLOW-UP ACTIVITIES

Ask students to

- Draw what they would like to be someday. Have them write or tell about their picture.
- Design a poster advertising the auditions to be held at the Performing Art Studio of _____ (your school's name).
- Write a play script for a favorite story line or one scene from a story. Perform the script.
- Read a play script and critique.
- Write a group or individual critique for a movie or a video.
- Be a reviewer and write to a classmate to tell him or her what you liked about his or her audition.

AUDITION SCRIPTS

Use the entire suggested script for older students, but use only the italic sections for younger students.

Cinderella

I wish I were going to the ball. I just can't believe I wasn't invited to the ball. I don't care what it takes to get there, even if I have to go in rags.

Peter Pan

I can fly. Won't you come and fly with me?

Wolf

These pigs are not very smart. I can blow down their houses with one little puff.

Chicken Little

Help! Help! Help! The sky is falling. All of you come with me to tell the king. Hurry!

Little Old Woman

I've had it with this shoe. There is just not enough room for all the children, and I have no room to cook a decent meal.

Humpty Dumpty

I know I've been told to stay off this wall, but sitting on this wall gives me a better view. Stop pushing me! *Oh no! I'm falling.*

Teacher's Script for Rumplestiltskin

The miller's daughter does not know my name. Tomorrow I will claim her child. She will never know my name. I am Rumplestiltskin.

STORY DRAMA

"AT THE CROSSROADS"

Based on the book by Rachel Isadora
(Life in a small village without material comforts)

When introducing this book it is important to give the students some background information about the setting of the story. The following is an example.

This story probably takes place in an African village. The village does not have factories, malls, or office buildings. Many fathers have to leave home to work. The fathers in this village work in mines far from the village, so they cannot come home every day. These mines might contain gold or diamonds. The people in this village are poor. They do not have running water in their homes, TVs, or computer games to play. But, the children are just like you. They go to school. They play. They have friends, and they miss their fathers.

The fathers have been away working at the mines. The mothers, children, and other villagers await their return. As the wait gets longer and longer, some villagers return home. Six children wait through the dark to be the first to greet their fathers.

> **TEACHER AS VILLAGER:** We all live in a small village in Africa. Many of our fathers are gone working in the mines. We have not met everyone in our village. My name is Rachel MaryLouise. I am the seamstress for our village. I've sewn many garments for all of you, but never met you.

Ask for volunteers to introduce themselves to the rest of the villagers. They are to tell their names and what they do in the village. (Hint: Remember students' roles so you can direct questions to them in their roles as the drama develops.)

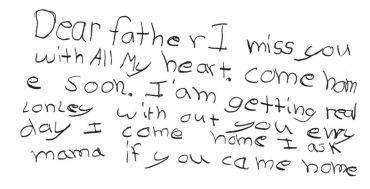

From *Story Dramas*, published by Good Year Books. Copyright © 1997 Sarah Jossart & Gretchen Courtney.

Read aloud the first page. (Pages are not numbered.)

TEACHER AS VILLAGER (*questioning students in the roles of the village children*):

What kind of mine does your father work in?

What do you miss the most about your father?

What will your father notice that is different about you when he returns?

How have you helped your mother and the rest of the village?

TEACHER AS VILLAGER (*questioning students playing the roles of village women*):

What foods are you preparing for the fathers' return?

What is the hardest part of having the fathers gone?

What do you hope the fathers will bring home?

TEACHER AS VILLAGER (*questioning students playing older men and fathers left in the village*):

What jobs in the village have you had to do for the fathers that are gone?

What do you remember about your times away at the mines?

Why aren't you in the mines?

Read aloud pages 2–3.

TEACHER AS VILLAGER (*questioning students in their previous roles*):

Women, what are you talking about at the well?

Children, what conversations have you overheard at the well?

Men, what news did you tell at the well?

Read aloud pages 4–7.

TEACHER AS VILLAGER (*questioning those in the role of children*):

What will school be like today?

What do you think the teacher will have you do to prepare for your fathers' return?

How will you concentrate?

Do you think you'll get out of school early? Why or why not?

From *Story Dramas*, published by Good Year Books. Copyright © 1997 Sarah Jossart & Gretchen Courtney.

Read aloud pages 8–17.

Have students form small groups and plan a pantomime of some activity they can do as they wait for the fathers to return. Then have them perform their ideas for the rest of the class.

Read aloud pages 18–19.

TEACHER AS VILLAGER *(questioning all students in their roles)*:

Who is going home and why?

Who is staying and why?

If you stay, what will you do now?

Read aloud pages 20–21.

TEACHER AS VILLAGER *(questioning all students in the role of children)*:

How are you feeling?

Why won't you go home?

What do you think your mother is doing at home?

What does your mother think about you not coming home?

Does your mother understand why you are not coming home?

Why do you think the others went home?

Read aloud pages 22–27.

TEACHER AS VILLAGER *(continuing to question)*:

Why hasn't your father come?

Will you keep waiting? Why or why not?

Are you sure he didn't come during the night and miss you? Why or why not?

What is the hardest thing about waiting?

Read aloud page 28 through to the end of the story.

FOLLOW-UP ACTIVITIES

Ask students to

- Pretend they are writing a letter to their fathers who are away working in the mines. What would each of them tell about his or her life at home in the village?
- Make a group or individual list of ways they can help their mothers and/or fathers.
- Write a journal entry about their life in the village.
- Draw a picture showing how they can help their mothers and fathers.
- Find out more about what their parents do at work. Ask them to tell the class.

STORY DRAMA

"IN THE MONTH OF KISLEV: A STORY OF HANUKKAH"

Based on the book by Nina Jaffe
(A holiday story about sharing)

This story shares some of the customs and traditions of the Jewish holiday Hanukkah. The text tells a universal story of sharing. The nonfiction information at the end of the story gives the reader background information regarding the significance of the holiday.

Read aloud pages 6–9.

TEACHER AS THE MAYOR: Hi, my name is Mr. Weiss. I am the mayor of our town. I've been so busy I haven't had time to meet you, the people of the village. Please introduce yourself to the rest of the town. Tell us your name and what you do in our town.

Have students volunteer to introduce themselves.

TEACHER AS THE MAYOR (*questioning students in their roles*):
How long have you lived in our town?
How long have you been a customer of Mendel?
What trinkets have you bought from him?
How has Mendel treated you?
How long have you been Feivel's customer?
What lumber product did you buy from him?
How has Feivel treated you?
Have you ever asked Feivel for anything? What have you asked him for?

Read aloud pages 10–11.

TEACHER AS THE MAYOR (*questioning students in their roles*):
How are you getting ready for Hanukkah?
Describe the latkes (potato pancakes). How do they taste?
How many copper coins did you get? What will you do with them?

Read aloud pages 12–15. Ask students to pretend they are Mendel, Rivkah, or one of the other children.

TEACHER AS THE MAYOR (*questioning students in the roles of Mendel, Rivkah, or one of the children*):
How are you feeling? Why?
What do you want to be different?
Why are you children smiling?
Why do you parents think the children are smiling?
What do you think the Hanukkah miracle might be?

Read aloud pages 16–19.

From *Story Dramas*, published by Good Year Books. Copyright © 1997 Sarah Jossart & Gretchen Courtney.

> **TEACHER AS THE MAYOR** *(questioning as above):*
> How are you feeling now? Why?
> What do you want to say to Feivel?
> What do you want to tell the Rabbi?
> Do you think you should pay a fine? Why or why not?
> What do you hope the Rabbi will decide?

Read aloud pages 20–22, stopping after the second paragraph on page 22.

> **TEACHER AS THE MAYOR** *(to students as original townspeople):* Townspeople, look for the Hanukkah gelt. Let's all check our pants pockets. *(Pause.)* Check your shirt pockets. *(Pause.)* Now count the coins you've found. *(Pause.)* Decide what you will give to the Rabbi. As I come around, drop your coins into this bag. *(Passes around a small, brown paper lunch bag. As each student pretends to put in a coin, snaps fingers against the side of the bag to make a noise that sounds like something dropping in the bag.)*

Read aloud from the third paragraph on page 22 through page 25.

> **TEACHER AS THE MAYOR** *(questioning townspeople):*
> What is the Rabbi doing?
> What do you think is going to happen?
> Will Feivel get his money? Why or why not?

Read aloud pages 26–27.

> **TEACHER AS THE MAYOR** *(continuing to question students):*
> Do you think the Rabbi was wise? Why or why not?
> How would you have solved the problem?
> Will Feivel change his ways? Why or why not?

Read aloud pages 28–31.

From *Story Dramas*, published by Good Year Books. Copyright © 1997 Sarah Jossart & Gretchen Courtney.

FOLLOW-UP ACTIVITIES

Ask students to

- List traditions of a Hanukkah holiday.
- Draw a picture about a holiday they enjoy celebrating, and then write or tell about it.
- Make a list of things their families do to get ready for a holiday.
- Make latkes and write about the experience.
- Listen to or read these other books about Hanukkah: *Light the Light!* by Margaret Moorman, *Count the Days of Hanukkah,* by Gail Herman, and *Hanukkah,* by Roni Schotter.
- Pretend to be one of the children on page 13 and write what they might be thinking or saying.

Recipe for Latkes

(German family recipe)

1 quart grated potatoes
3 eggs, beaten
salt
1/4 cup cream
4 tablespoons flour

Add beaten eggs, salt, and cream to bowl of grated potatoes and stir until mixed evenly. Stir in flour. Fry in a well-greased pan.

STORY DRAMA

"SUN SONG"

Based on the book by Jean Marzollo
(A new day, told in verse)

Young students love the sun. We've all seen suns in their drawings. This circle story, told in verse, begins and ends with the beginning of a new day. The sun warms, touches, and dries the world of nature. The beautiful illustrations should be shared during this drama.

This text works very well for early literacy instruction. After the drama and an uninterrupted rereading of the text, you may use this as a reading lesson. Using copied phrases from several pages of the text on strips of paper, the students can sort out the phrase strips to match the text.

The morning greeting on the first page of text provides an extension into the classroom by becoming a morning greeting for several days. The class can continue this practice of morning greetings.

> **TEACHER AS NATURE GUIDE:** Welcome to Snow Village Farm. It is five o'clock in the morning. We are meeting here at Snow Village Farm for a day in the country. We are here this early in the morning because we want to observe the sun coming up, plant life in the early morning, and the morning animals. I am Ms. Valley, your nature guide. Before we begin our walk around the ranch, we would like to meet you. Tell us your name, where you are from, and what you hope to see or hear this morning at Snow Village Farm.

Ask for volunteers to introduce themselves. They are to tell their name, where they are from, and what they hope to see at the farm.

> **TEACHER AS NATURE GUIDE** (questioning students in their roles):
> What time did you get up to get here so early?
> Who came with you?
> How did you come?
> How did you hear about Snow Village Farm?
> What have you heard about Snow Village Farm?
> What sounds do you hope to hear today?
> What equipment, besides a camera, did you bring along? Why?
> What do you think the sun song would sound like?

> **TEACHER AS NATURE GUIDE:** Ladies and gentlemen, I am asking you to face the east to watch the sun rise. (*Has students turn to face the east.*)

Read aloud the first four lines on the first page of text. (Pages have no numbers so refer to pages with text only.) Ask for volunteers to describe the sunrise they see.

From *Story Dramas*, published by Good Year Books. Copyright © 1997 Sarah Jossart & Gretchen Courtney.

TEACHER AS NATURE GUIDE: As we walk through the farm it will be important that we remain quiet so as not to disturb the animals. Please do not feed the animals or pick the plants.

Read aloud the rest of the first page through the fourth text page, showing the pictures as you read.

TEACHER AS NATURE GUIDE (*questioning students in their roles*):
What have you seen so far that has interested you?
What have you liked the best of the animals we have seen? Why?
What special thing did you notice about the fawn, turtle, mole, sheep, horse, or the robin?

(Note: Skip page of text about the boy waking up, found on page five.) Read aloud text pages 6–11.

TEACHER AS NATURE GUIDE (*questioning students in their roles*):
What pictures have you taken?
What sounds have you heard?
What other observations have you made during your nature walk?
If you haven't seen or heard what you had hoped, do you feel disappointed? Why or why not?
Where will you go to see or hear that special thing?
What would you go back to see again? Why?
What special animal or plant did you see that no one else saw?
Describe what you saw.

TEACHER AS NATURE GUIDE: We are coming to the end of the day. The time has gone by so quickly. Can you believe we have been out all day looking around Snow Village Farm? Ladies and gentleman, please turn toward the west to watch the setting sun. (*Has the students face west.*) Do you see the oranges, blues, and pinks of the sunset? Does the sunset you see have other colors? What color do you see the most of? (*Pause.*) The sun is sinking lower and lower in the sky. It is behind the trees. (*Pause.*) And now it has slipped beyond the horizon. Another day is done.

Read aloud pages 12 and 13 and pause. Then read aloud the last page of text.

FOLLOW-UP ACTIVITIES

Ask students to

- Make a drawing of something they might see on a nature walk.
- Write or draw an observational journal of an animal or plant brought into the classroom for actual observation.
- Write a group "sun song." Try to put the ideas down to the tune of a familiar song.
- Write a list of things they like about the morning or a list of good ways to start a new day.
- Make a list of good things the sun does.
- Study the sun and learn some facts about the sun.
- Write about a personal experience of getting up early.
- Listen to the book *The Way to Start a Day,* by Byrd Baylor, and discuss it.
- Listen to or read these circle stories: *Like Butter on Pancakes,* by Jonathan London, and *The Good Night Circle,* by Carolyn Lesser.
- Brainstorm and list other words to describe the actions of the sun.

STORY DRAMA

"THE RAG COAT"

Based on the book by Lauren Mills
(A coat made by the community teaches love and friendship.)

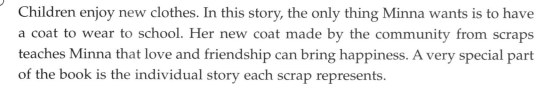

Children enjoy new clothes. In this story, the only thing Minna wants is to have a coat to wear to school. Her new coat made by the community from scraps teaches Minna that love and friendship can bring happiness. A very special part of the book is the individual story each scrap represents.

Students may not be familiar with the use of leftover cloth, or rags, for the making of quilts, coats, and other items. If possible, bring in a quilted item so they can see how the fabrics are all different, how little the pieces can be, and how they are put together.

Some students can relate to this story. These students may not have winter coats of their own or are in situations where their clothing needs are barely being met. Be prepared to handle a discussion of this sort if a student shares his or her situation.

From *Story Dramas,* published by Good Year Books. Copyright © 1997 Sarah Jossart & Gretchen Courtney.

Read aloud to the students the first four pages of text. (Pages are not numbered.)

> **TEACHER AS NEIGHBOR:** We are all neighbors of Minna and her family. We have lived in these mountains for years, but unless there is a special occasion or a death we never seem to get together. I am Mrs. Roth. I run the small store down by the corner road at the foot of the mountain. Each of you can introduce yourself to the rest of the neighbors. Tell the group your name, what you do on the mountain, and one thing you remember about Minna and Clemmie's father.

Ask for volunteers to introduce themselves and answer the questions above.

> **TEACHER AS NEIGHBOR** (questioning students in their roles):
> Where is Minna's home from where you live?
> How did you get here?
> Who came with you?
> What food did you bring? Why did you decide on that food?
> Why are you wearing black?

Read aloud the fifth page of text. Then ask students to pretend to be Minna.

> **TEACHER AS NEIGHBOR** (asking students, in their role of Minna):
> What are you thinking?
> Why do you want to go to school?
> What do you think you are missing at school?
> Do you see how your problem could be solved?
> What could you do to get a coat?
> Why don't you just ask your mother for a coat?

Have students form small groups and come up with an idea or solution to help Minna get a coat so she can go to school. Ask them to discuss and then share ideas.

Read aloud text pages 6–10.

TEACHER AS NEIGHBOR *(to students still in the role of Minna)*:
  How are you feeling at this point?
  What will you share about your coat?
  What do you think the teacher will say?
  What do you think the other students will say?
  What will you tell them about the feed-sack lining?
  Will you be able to sleep tonight? Why or why not?
  What do you think you will dream about?

Read aloud text pages 11 and 12.

TEACHER AS NEIGHBOR *(to students still in the role of Minna)*:
  What will you do when you get back to school?
  What will you tell your teacher?
  How are you feeling at this point? Why?
  What do you think of Lottie, Clyde, and Souci?

Read aloud text pages 13 and 14.

FOLLOW-UP ACTIVITIES

Ask students to

- Design a fabric scrap for the rag coat on a four-inch square piece of paper. Then write or tell the story behind the scrap of fabric.
- Write the story behind a real scrap of fabric from home. This could be part of a baby blanket, favorite stuffed toy, or article of clothing.
- Collect scraps of fabric and think of a story behind one scrap. Then share these stories in a storytelling time.
- Pretend they are Minna and write a group or individual thank-you note to Shane or Souci.
- Listen to *A New Coat for Anna*, by Harriet Ziefert, and discuss it.
- Plan a day when parents can come in and share the stories behind their quilted items.

From *Story Dramas*, published by Good Year Books. Copyright © 1997 Sarah Jossart & Gretchen Courtney.

STORY DRAMA

"THE RELATIVES CAME"

Based on the book by Cynthia Rylant
(A family reunion)

Relatives make a long journey through the mountains and across the country, coming up from Virginia to visit their family. They stay for weeks and weeks, but no one minds as they eat and breathe together. When the time comes for them to leave, everyone has something to remember.

Memories of the anticipated arrival of relatives rushes to mind as this book is read. What student hasn't felt some anticipation when his or her relatives are due to arrive?

This story drama begins with a family reunion—a big family reunion! Students play the roles, from tiny babies to 100-year-old men; they play the famous and the not-so-famous; some have prestigious jobs and some don't work at all. These imagined relatives have traveled from places all over the world and even out of this world. (Once students start creating characters, you can't stop them. Being from another country might not be enough.) Scenes of memorable moments with relatives are shared, such as times spent playing games, "cruising" the mall, fishing, and talking fashion.

"Snapshots" (student drawings) are taken to help remember this reunion and the relatives. "Photographs" of new relatives (drawings or pictures from magazines) can generate a lot of giggles. Journals, diaries, and letters written after the reunion are filled with feelings and memories.

Prepare a banner or write across the blackboard: WELCOME TO THE UBADA FAMILY REUNION _____ (insert current year).

Aunt Betty went to my house and when she went to my house she hug me then hug too tight then almost squish me like a bug.

> **TEACHER AS CAROL UBADA:** Welcome to the Ubada family reunion. It has been such a long time since our family has gotten together. *(Moves around the room and shakes a few hands, greeting relatives.)* I hardly recognize most of you, and I'm sure I can't remember many of you by name. I've heard so many stories about all of you and what exciting adventures you have had. I think we should really get acquainted with each other. I am Carol Ubada. I'm here with my family; those two boys playing baseball over by the oak tree are my boys.

Have students form pairs and interview each other. (You may need to model an interview.) Ask them to find out the relative's name, where the relative lives, about his or her job, family, and so on. Find out how the relative got to the reunion. Tell them to ask any questions that will help them get to know this relative better.

Ask for volunteers to introduce a relative to the rest of the relatives.

> **TEACHER AS CAROL UBADA:** It's so good to know you, but it seems one family is missing. I'd heard our relatives from Virginia, the ones that grow grapes, haven't arrived yet. *(Questions students in their roles.)*
> Does anyone remember this family?
> What are their names?
> How were they coming?
> Does anyone have an idea when they will arrive?
> Has anyone heard from them?
> What have you heard?

Read aloud pages 1–7. (Number all pages starting with the first page of text.)

> **TEACHER AS CAROL UBADA:** They're coming! I can see them, can you?
> *(Questions students in their roles.)*
> What will you say to them first?
> What will you do first?
> What will you want to show them?
> What will you want to tell them about you or another relative you've just met?

Read aloud pages 8–11.

TEACHER AS CAROL UBADA (*questioning students in their roles*):

How many hugs did you get?

Who had the tightest hug?

Did any of you hug Aunt Betty? What did you think of her hug?

Did you like the hugs? Why or why not?

Read aloud pages 12 and 13.

TEACHER AS CAROL UBADA (*questioning students in their roles*):

What did you have to eat?

Whom did you eat with?

What was the best food? the worst?

What food did you prepare, and why?

TEACHER IN NEW ROLE OF A NEIGHBOR: I am a neighbor, and I've just come over to see what all the noise, fun, and excitement is about. You all look like you are having so much fun. Wow, can your relatives visit! I don't mean to be snoopy, but can you tell me what all of you are talking about? (*Goes around asking volunteers to tell about their conversations. Questions them as needed.*) This has been interesting. It was great hearing about _____ (*highlights some of the conversations shared*). I've been wondering how you will all sleep tonight. (*Questions relatives concerning what plans have been made for sleeping.*)

Does anyone have extra pillows, blankets?

Are there any volunteers to sleep in a tent? Why or why not?

Would you sleep under the stars? Why or why not? in a motel? on the floor?

Do you know of any relative that sleepwalks or snores?

Read aloud pages 14–21.

Have students form small groups of three or four and plan an activity they might do with relatives. Ask them to prepare a pantomime to share, showing activities such as shopping, playing a game, swimming, and so on. Each group can share their pantomime.

Read aloud pages 22–26.

TEACHER AS A RELATIVE: All of us have left the family reunion. We're all back in our own homes. It's a nice, cozy evening, and we're thinking about last summer's reunion and dreaming about next year. What was the highlight of the Ubada reunion? What experience will you never forget? what relative? what else?

FOLLOW-UP ACTIVITIES

Ask students to

- Write or tell about the reunion, an interesting relative they've met, the activities at the reunion, and so on.
- Draw a "photograph" of some activity at the reunion, then write a description of the "photo."
- Write about plans they would make for next year's reunion. This writing could be in the form of a journal, letter, story, and so on.
- Pretend they are a Virginia relative and write a group or individual thank-you letter.
- Write or tell about a picture of a person cut from a magazine. Pretend this person is a new relative and make a class "family" photo album.
- Draw the "photo" of a relative they met and write about this person. These pretend photos could also be put in a family photo album.
- Write a story about an old photograph. (Hint: You can locate photographs in antique stores and garage sales, or you could use some of your own old family pictures. Make a photocopy of these photographs so you can use them over and over again without destroying them.)

From *Story Dramas*, published by Good Year Books. Copyright © 1997 Sarah Jossart & Gretchen Courtney.

GENRE
HISTORICAL FICTION

Historical fiction introduces students to periods of history we can only visit through visual or auditory media. We use historical fiction to introduce students to the past, informing them about the ways people lived, loved, played, and solved problems. Good historical fiction must be accurate, because young students often have little prior knowledge of the historical reference. Students also use historical fiction to learn facts that support their studies in learning content areas such as history and social science.

STORY DRAMA
"THE FIRST THANKSGIVING"

Based on the book by Jean Craighead George
(Retelling of the first Thanksgiving)

The First Thanksgiving is one of the most beautiful books ever created. The carefully crafted words of Jean Craighead George and the colorful, complex paintings of Thomas Locker join together in this masterful retelling of the New World's first Thanksgiving. This book, read aloud, creates a sense of "being there" for the students. The language is quite rich and descriptive. Even the younger students become involved in the telling of the tale and the beauty of the illustrations.

The drama begins late in the text when the students have been immersed in the sights, sounds, and emotions of this time. Older students may have more background knowledge to add to the drama. The telling of the Thanksgiving story is never untimely, but this drama has special impact just preceding the Thanksgiving holiday.

Read pages 1–16 aloud, showing all the illustrations. (The pages are not numbered.)

Dear cousin,
How are you? I like it in the new world. an indin named Squanto. He taught us how to fish, grow corn and we picked berries, we are geting lots of food, good bye!

Sincerly,

TEACHER AS JOHN MACOMB: My heart feels heavy at the sight of the *Mayflower* sailing into the deep ocean. She was a home to me, John Macomb, and my family. Luckily, my family has survived thus far, and now, with hard work and neighborly help, we shall all survive in this strange, new home. As I look around I see all of you, my fellow travelers, ready to settle on this lonely coastal shore. *(Begins to walk around the room, stopping to ask students the following questions.)*

How do you feel about the *Mayflower* leaving?

Is your family with you?

What are you able to do to help us all survive in this land?

Tell us your name and about the family you have with you.

TEACHER AS JOHN MACOMB: We have gathered here this evening in the common house to write down the rules and laws that will govern our small community. Without each other's help, we will not survive in this land. I am glad to see each and every one of you. Every person's voice is important in the laws of our land.

Have students form small groups and write down the rules and laws they think will help their small community survive and stay in harmony. Then share ideas with the whole class and create a combined list of rules and laws for the Pilgrim community.

Read aloud pages 17–24.

TEACHER AS JOHN MACOMB: Squanto has become a true and loyal friend. He taught me how to plant my corn so that the stalks grow strong and tall. He has shared with me the secrets of the things to eat that grow in the forest land. He has shown me how to make leather for shoes from the soft skin of the deer. I am truly grateful for his help.

Have students pretend they are Pilgrims. Tell them Squanto has helped each and every one of them discover helpful and wonderful things about this land on which they now live. Ask them to write a letter home to a friend or relative explaining all of the things Squanto has taught them and how it has helped them survive in this land far away from England.

Read aloud pages 25–28.

From *Story Dramas*, published by Good Year Books. Copyright © 1997 Sarah Jossart & Gretchen Courtney.

Ask students to find themselves in the picture on pages 27 and 28. In small groups, have them plan and act out a short scene from this day. They may be helping to cook and serve all of the food, playing a game, participating in a sport with the Indian guests, even hunting in the woods for more food to cook for the ninety Indian guests and all of the Pilgrim community. Have them share their short skits with the rest of the class.

Read aloud the last page of the book.

FOLLOW-UP ACTIVITIES
Ask students to
- Pretend they are a pilgrim and write a diary entry beginning the day the *Mayflower* set sail until the day of the great celebration.
- Draw or paint a scene from the Thanksgiving celebration, copying the style or colors used by Thomas Locker.
- Compare your celebration of the Thanksgiving holiday with the Pilgrims'.
- Rewrite the Pilgrims' landing in the New World and the Thanksgiving celebration from the Indians' point of view.
- Enact the Thanksgiving feast, with everyone taking different roles. Sit in groups and share popcorn and apple slices.

STORY DRAMA

"AMBER ON THE MOUNTAIN"

Based on the book by Tony Johnston
(A child's wish to read and write comes true.)

Children take the privilege of going to school as an everyday occurrence, but for Amber this is not the case. Amber wants to learn to read and write, but she has no school to help her. Her friend, Anna, introduces her to the wonders of literacy. Amber is hooked; she wants to be part of this new and wonderful literate world. Amber's desire to learn to read and write gives students a fresh look at the personal drive to learn.

Amber is my best friend.
Cousin Amber likes to play with me

Read aloud the first page of text. (Pages are not numbered. The number of the page will refer only to the pages with text.)

TEACHER AS MOUNTAIN DWELLER *(to students):* Imagine this mountain with me. It is very large and high. It is covered with trees. The top of the mountain is often covered with fog, and early in the fall snow will begin to cover its peak. Dirt trails connect the homes on this mountain with the rest of the world. We are the people who live on this mountain. Our homes are scattered all over this mountain, and we have not had the chance to meet one another. I am Jack Dohrman. I live on the north side of this mountain, on a cattle ranch. I love the wide open spaces here. Tell us your name, where you live on this mountain, and one thing you like about your mountain home.

Have students, pretending to be mountain dwellers, volunteer to introduce themselves to the rest of the group.

TEACHER AS MOUNTAIN DWELLER *(questioning students in their roles):*
   Are you lonesome like Amber? Why or why not?
   What do you think of mountain air?
   Do you get many visitors? Why or why not?
   When was the last time you saw a neighbor?
   Where do you get your supplies?
   Do you have a school? Why not?
   Have you learned to read and write? Why not?
   Do you know Amber?
   What do you think of Amber?

Read aloud the second page.

From *Story Dramas*, published by Good Year Books. Copyright © 1997 Sarah Jossart & Gretchen Courtney.

TEACHER AS MOUNTAIN DWELLER *(continuing to question students in their roles):*

    What can you tell us about the teacher that left?

    Did you ever meet this teacher? What did you think of him?

    What part of mountain life do you think was too hard for the teacher?

    How did you feel when he left?

    What can you tell us about the man building the road?

    Do you agree with Granny Cotton's thoughts about the road? Why or why not?

    Do you think the road will get built? Why or why not?

Read aloud pages 3–5.

Have students form small groups and make a list of things they would do to help teach someone to read. (In kindergarten and early first grade, you might wish to do this as a class by asking the students to think of what is helping them learn about reading. List their ideas on the board.)

Read aloud pages 6–9. Then ask students to pretend they are Anna.

TEACHER AS MOUNTAIN DWELLER *(questioning students in the role of Anna):*

    How do you feel, now that Amber can read?

    From the list of ideas, which idea do you think helped her learn to read? Why?

    Why do you want to teach Amber to write?

    How will you teach her to write?

    Who taught you to write?

TEACHER AS MOUNTAIN DWELLER *(questioning students in the role of Amber):*

    How do you feel now that you can read?

    What made learning to read hard or easy for you?

    What do you enjoy about reading?

    From the list of ideas, which idea do you think helped you learn to read? Why?

    Do you want to learn to write? Why or why not?

Read aloud pages 10–11. Then ask students to pretend they are Amber.

TEACHER AS MOUNTAIN DWELLER *(questioning students in the role of Amber):*
What will you do to learn to write?
Who will you get to help you?

Read aloud pages 12–14 up to the letter on page 14.

Students should continue in the role of Amber and write a group or individual letter to Anna. Ask them to share letters with the rest of the class.

Starting on page 14, read aloud the letter and page 15.

FOLLOW-UP ACTIVITIES

Ask students to

• Write a narrative about their experiences learning to read and write.
• Write a letter to a friend or relative and mail it.
• Make a class list of strategies students use to help them read and write.
• Draw a picture of their school.
• Ask their parents how they learned to read and write and who taught them.

STORY DRAMA

"WATCH THE STARS COME OUT"

Based on the book by Riki Levinson
(A grandmother tells the story of her mother's journey to America.)

Children today may know very little about the immigration period between 1892 and 1954. In this story, a grandmother tells the story of her mother's journey to America. She is telling the story to a child of the second generation. Storytelling has traditionally been the way favorite stories about families have been preserved. This text is a good example of a family storytelling.

From *Story Dramas*, published by Good Year Books. Copyright © 1997 Sarah Jossart & Gretchen Courtney.

Children are oftentimes interested in their heritage after hearing this story. You might encourage them to discuss their heritage with their family and also encourage parents to pass down stories to their children. Perhaps one of your students will discover he or she is one of the more than 100 million Americans who can trace family roots to someone who came to America by way of Ellis Island.

Twelve million immigrants were welcomed to America by way of Ellis Island, New York, between the years of 1892 and 1954. The immigrants arrived after a sea voyage of eight to more than twenty days. They paid thirty-five dollars each for the voyage. They came wearing identification tags, carrying passports, and lugging their belongings in trunks of many makes and sizes.

Upon the immigrants' arrival at Ellis Island, the waiting began. There were long lines for processing. Each immigrant was given a medical examination. If doctors discovered a disease such as measles, the immigrant was not allowed to be processed until the disease was cured. Immigrants found to have contagious eye infections, lameness, and mental illnesses would be sent back to their homeland. Once the medical examination was passed, there was an interview with many questions to be answered: What is your age? Where do you plan to live? What job do you have arranged? What job do you plan to get? How much money do you have?

Immigrants today are prescreened and approved by the U.S. Embassy. It takes only a few minutes to be processed. Three identifying features are recorded: a photograph of the face taken at an angle to show the right earlobe, a print of the right index finger, and a signature.

Children will enjoy other stories of immigration: *How Many Days to America? A Thanksgiving Story,* by Mazinne Rhea Leighton; *I Hate English!* by Ellen Levine; *Molly's Pilgrim,* by Barbara Cohen; *Soon Annala,* by Riki Levinson; and *Immigrant Girl: Becky of Eldridge Street,* by Brett Harvey.

Read the title, *Watch the Stars Come Out,* to the class. Have the students predict what the story might be about. Who might the people on the cover be? What do you think they are carrying, and what are they doing?

Read aloud pages 2–3. (Skip page 1. Pages are not numbered.)

From *Story Dramas,* published by Good Year Books. Copyright © 1997 Sarah Jossart & Gretchen Courtney.

TEACHER AS CAPTAIN BLACKWELL: Welcome aboard the New World Ship. I am Captain Blackwell, and I will be in charge of this ship for your journey. We will be traveling westward at twenty knots. The sea is reported to be calm with waves of four to six feet. You will be traveling with many other people, and to make your trip more pleasant you will have the chance to meet some of your fellow passengers.

Have students form pairs and interview each other to learn their partners' names, where they are from, whom they are traveling with, and why they are going to America. Ask for volunteers to introduce their partners to the rest of the class.

TEACHER AS CAPTAIN BLACKWELL (questioning students in their roles):

What will you do in America?

What special item did you pack to bring to America? Why is that item so special? Describe the item.

What did you have to leave behind? Why?

Who will you meet in America?

Are you looking forward to this trip? Why or why not?

Is your whole family traveling with you? Why or why not?

Read aloud pages 4–9.

TEACHER AS CAPTAIN BLACKWELL (questioning students in their roles):

How is your trip going?

What can I, your captain, do to make it a better trip for you?

What do you do every day to keep busy on the ship?

What is the hardest part of the trip so far? Why?

What do you miss the most?

Do you miss the stars too? Why or why not?

Did you know the old lady who died? What can you tell me about her?

Do you know how long you've been on this ship?

How much more time do you think it will be before we get to America?

How are you keeping track of time?

How will you know when we get to America?

From *Story Dramas,* published by Good Year Books. Copyright © 1997 Sarah Jossart & Gretchen Courtney.

Have students form small groups and pretend the trip is getting long. Ask them to make a list of activities for adults and students to help make the time go more quickly. Students should share their group's ideas with the rest of the class.

Read aloud pages 10–11.

TEACHER (*questioning students in their roles*):

Why is everyone so excited?

How are you feeling?

What are you waving at? How do you know it is the Statue of Liberty?

Did you wave to the statue? Why or why not?

What do you see in the distance? Describe what you see.

What does this all mean to you?

What will happen next?

Do you have any fears? Why or why not?

What fears do you have?

Read aloud pages 12–17.

TEACHER AS MEMBER OF WELCOMING COMMITTEE: Ladies, gentlemen, boys, and girls, welcome to America. I am here to greet you and see if I can be of any help to you. (*Goes around questioning the students as passengers.*)

Do you see anyone you know?

Tell me one thing you'll never forget about your trip.

What do you plan to do in America?

What kind of job do you hope to get?

Do you have a place to stay?

Are you planning on staying in New York or going on? Where might you go?

Do you have any questions about America I could answer for you? (*Encourages the students to ask questions new immigrants might ask their first day in America.*)

Read aloud pages 18–27. (Skip the last page.)

TEACHER *(questioning students in their roles):*

What are you thinking about your first night in America?

What will you do the first thing in the morning? Why?

What advice would you give someone who might be just starting their journey to America?

What part of this trip will you remember to tell your children and grandchildren?

FOLLOW-UP ACTIVITIES

Ask students to

- Write a newspaper article about newcomers to America.
- Write a personal journal entry about their trip to America.
- Write a journal entry for the captain of the ship.
- Draw a picture of what they would like their new home in America to look like. Write or tell about their picture.
- Draw a picture of what they think the boat looked like.
- Write a sequel to the story.
- Write The Convention and Visitors' Bureau (2 Columbus Circle, 59th Street, New York, NY 10019) for information about Ellis Island.
- Write or tell what America means to them today.
- Make a list of five things they must do as a newcomer to America. Try to prioritize this list.
- Write a recipe for a homemade food their family enjoys.
- Listen to a rereading of the story. Discuss family storytelling traditions.
- Ask their parents to tell them a family story.
- Discuss the inscription on the Statue of Liberty's pedestal:

  Give me your tired, your poor,

  Your huddled masses yearning to breathe free,

  The wretched refuse of your teeming shore;

  Send these, the homeless, tempest-tossed, to me:

  I lift my lamp beside the golden door.

- Research the process of becoming an American citizen.
- If possible, interview a new immigrant to this country. Plan questions they would ask in this interview.

From *Story Dramas*, published by Good Year Books. Copyright © 1997 Sarah Jossart & Gretchen Courtney.

STORY DRAMA

"GOING WEST"

Based on the book by Jean Van Leeuwen
(Pioneers cross the land hoping for a better life.)

The brief period of history from the early to mid 1800s, when people later known as pioneers crossed the land, is far removed from the experiences of students today. This book, told from a child's perspective, helps bring the sights, sounds, and images of that time into today's world. This is a story of a single family crossing from east to west. Hardships are plainly told and loneliness is portrayed as a way of life.

This book spans all four seasons, and the drama has students not only creating and changing characters, but also changing and creating within seasonal settings. Students become especially involved in being trapped inside during a winter storm.

The plain simple language of the text makes the book an excellent choice for primary students. *Cassie's Journey*, by Brett Harvey, works well as a companion piece, especially as a read-aloud.

This drama follows a family's travels from east to west and spans a year of their lives. The drama could take up to two hours if presented in one session, or it can be stopped where noted within the drama and continued the next day.

TEACHER AS NARRATOR: Look out the window. Do you see what I see? I see long, tall grass, as tall as my shoulders, growing as far as I can see without a tree in sight. Oh! Look over there, I see mounds and mounds of blue, pink, and purple flowers. Listen, I am sure I hear a creek flowing over rocks. The water makes such a pleasant sound. Take a deep breath; can you smell the flowers and the grass? This is such a lovely place. Would you like to go farther west? It is a very hard journey. There may be many dangers along the way. Let's go, all of us! Let's go west!

From *Story Dramas*, published by Good Year Books. Copyright © 1997 Sarah Jossart & Gretchen Courtney.

TEACHER AS MAMA: My name is Mary Walters. I have three children: Hannah, who is seven; Jake, who is five; and Rebecca, who is almost two and learning to talk. We are going west with my husband, John, to find a new prairie home and to build a farm as big as the sky. I am anxious about leaving; it may be difficult. All of you, my family, are excited to go. It is hard to leave behind so many of our belongings. Rebecca, where are you? Jake, Hannah, are you with the baby?

Have students take the role of Hannah, Jake, Rebecca, Mama, or Papa.

TEACHER AS NARRATOR: Today is the day your family is leaving to go west into the great prairie. I know you are all anxious to start this adventure. What are you looking forward to the most? *(Informally interviews students, finding out their identity and asking them the following questions.)*

Who will you miss here at home?

What will you leave behind because there isn't room in the wagon?

What types of dangers do you think are waiting for you on your journey?

Are you ready to go?

Do you want to move west? Why or why not?

Dear Nicholas,

How are you? I'm fine. We miss you. The land is beautiful here. We pray that out corn will make it this season. We had a bad storm last night. Why dont you come and visit some time? We would love to see you. Give our love to everybody. Write back soon.

Love,
Scott

From *Story Dramas*, published by Good Year Books. Copyright © 1997 Sarah Jossart & Gretchen Courtney.

Read aloud pages 1–8. (The pages are not numbered. Begin with the first page of text, numbering all pages.)

TEACHER AS MAMA: This spring has been the rainiest I can remember. It is so muddy and cold. This journey seems so long.

Read aloud pages 9–10.

TEACHER AS MAMA: I can hardly move. My arms are so tired from pushing the heavy wagon. The whole family is hungry, because I cannot cook over a fire when it is raining so hard. Little Rebecca has a cold, and there is no doctor for her to see. I never thought this journey would be so hard.

In small groups, have students talk about the most difficult part of this journey. Groups should share their thoughts with the whole class.

Read aloud the first two lines of page 11.

Have students think of ways they and their family can cross the river safely. Remember that this river is quite deep and is moving quickly downstream.

Read aloud the remainder of page 11 through page 14.

Ask students to draw a picture of what they think their house will look like.

Read aloud pages 15–28. (This is a good place to stop the drama if it is to be done in two sections.)

Tell students summer has arrived and the weather is hot and dry. Ask them to add to the drawings of their houses, showing what it looks like in the summer.

Have students form five groups: a group of Hannahs, Jakes, Mamas, Papas, and Rebeccas. Then ask them to make a list of all the things they need to do in the summer to get ready for the winter. Read each list aloud to the rest of the class.

Read aloud pages 29–30.

> **TEACHER AS MAMA:** I still miss my sisters so much. I haven't seen them for seven months now. I haven't even gotten one letter from them. I am going to write them right now and tell them about how different life is here on the prairie. I have to tell them about the time the Indians came. That was quite a day!

Ask students to take the role of either Mama or Papa and write a letter to someone she or he misses.

Read aloud pages 31–40.

Prompt students to think about what it is like to be inside during the winter when it is too snowy and icy to go anywhere. In their family role, have them think of ideas to help survive the long, cold winter. Share these ideas with the rest of the class.

Read aloud pages 41–45.

> **TEACHER AS NEIGHBOR:** Hello, hello, is there anybody home? I am Constance Weller. My husband, Carl Weller, and I are building a home about two miles away, down by the creek. We came here from Pennsylvania with our four boys, Joseph, Michael, Robert, and Luke. We are having a hard time getting our seeds to grow, with all the rain and all. We just drove our wagon over to meet you folks and ask you how to get a good crop in the ground.

In roles as new neighbors, have students introduce themselves and tell the rest of the community about themselves and their families.

> **TEACHER AS MAMA:** It seems like such a long time since we moved west, but really it has been only ten years. Little Hannah is married now with a baby of her own, and Rebecca is almost grown up. Jake is taller than his father and twice as strong. We have a whole town full of neighbors now, and it seems as if new people move in every day. I can see at least five houses from my front porch. I sometimes miss the days, ten years ago, when we were alone on the vast prairie lands. I wonder what will come to the prairie next.

From *Story Dramas*, published by Good Year Books. Copyright © 1997 Sarah Jossart & Gretchen Courtney.

FOLLOW-UP ACTIVITIES

Ask students to

- Write a sequel to *Going West* that takes place ten years later.
- Write or tell about a time when they were lonely.
- Write or tell about their favorite season.
- Compare the picture of the pioneer home drawn in the drama with their own home.
- Write a return letter to Mama or Papa.
- Listen to or read these two other westward movement books: *My Prairie Year,* by Brett Harvey, and *Pioneers,* by Martin W. Sandler.

SECTION 4

How to Construct Your Own Dramas: Step-By-Step

- **STORY AND TEXT SELECTION**

- **DRAMA CONSTRUCTION**

- **WRITING EXTENSIONS**

STORY AND TEXT SELECTION

The first step in the construction of a story drama is the selection of the story or text. A picture storybook with limited written material is a good choice, but also look beyond the picture storybooks and consider other age-appropriate materials, such as poetry, historical fiction, textbooks, newspaper or journal articles, and students' stories, as well as novels. If you want to use a longer piece, such as a novel, the drama can be written for various parts of the text, certain chapters, or selected pages or paragraphs. First read the entire text of the selected piece. Does it have the qualities of a good read-aloud? Does the natural flow of the text provide places to stop and improvise? If the answer is yes, continue with the text.

Certain characteristics need to be present in a piece of writing in order for it to become a good story drama. Look for the following five components when selecting your text:

1. Problem to solve: An integral part of a workable story drama is the opportunity for students to interact with each other in a problem-solving situation, while playing the role of a character. No problem is too great or too small to be tackled. Look for conflict between individuals or conflict within a character. Expand and examine conflict between humans and nature, such as survival, or conflict between humans and society, such as prejudice. To find solutions to the posed problem, each student must analyze the character he or she is portraying, using that character's unique talents or strengths to obtain solutions. Students must also use information about other characters portrayed by their classmates in the same way.

2. Opportunity for the development of additional characters: One of the goals in story drama is to immerse students in characterization. Providing an opportunity for students to develop their own characters does this well. Students not only control their choice and enjoy creating a character, but they must also evaluate the story setting and other story characters when molding their characters. Look for places in your text to add neighbors, crowd situations, city officials, reporters, family members, pets, animals, townspeople, garbage men, painters, and so on.

3. Interesting story characters: To achieve the goal of developing in students a keen eye for evaluating characters, they must be exposed to a diversity of characters in multiple texts. A student will incorporate character traits he or she has experienced in stories when developing his or her own character's traits.

From Story Dramas, published by Good Year Books. Copyright © 1997 Sarah Jossart & Gretchen Courtney.

4. Opportunity to predict: Students use their knowledge of many literary elements when they predict what will happen next in a story. They rely even more on that prior knowledge when they role-play their predictions. Just imagine the higher-level thinking that takes place when your students think through setting, plot, theme, characters, and mood before making a good prediction. When you are looking for places in the text to stop and ask for predictions, evaluate natural turning points in the story.

5. Well-written, age-appropriate text and enriched vocabulary: Here again, provide good examples for your students. One of the natural effects of story drama is that students incorporate the vocabulary of the text into their role-playing, predicting, problem-solving, and writing. Choosing a text with a rich vocabulary and linguistic merit will benefit your students in many ways—the least of which is that the story drama will be much more interesting.

Text Selection Checklist

1. Problem to solve

2. Opportunity for the development of additional characters

3. Interesting story characters

4. Opportunity to predict

5. Well-written, age-appropriate text and enriched vocabulary

DRAMA CONSTRUCTION

After you have selected one or two stories or other texts that you enjoy and you feel are workable, it is time to begin the second step, drama construction. Do not be discouraged or alarmed if you start the construction process and find that the particular piece you are working with is becoming thorny, and you are forcing the process rather than it occurring naturally. It's fine to stop, use that piece for another purpose, and go on to your next selection. Each drama you write will become easier, and you will find that soon you have a pile of books stacked up on your desk that are just perfect for dramas.

Read the entire text. To begin story drama construction, read the entire text. Even though you may be using only parts of the text, an entire reading may spark some ideas for you to incorporate into your drama. As you are reading, focus on these five elements that form the backbone of a well-composed story drama: role-playing situations, problem(s) to be solved, character development and interaction, open-ended questions, and written-language responses.

Model role-playing and provide role-playing opportunities. To begin your drama, establish a role-playing situation early. You should choose a role first, and often this role is the springboard for the other roles. Keep in mind that you may want to have many role-playing situations in your drama. Sometimes role-playing begins before the actual reading of the story. For example, in the "Humpty Dumpty" drama on pp. 8–10, the teacher begins by taking a role and involving the students in new roles before any text is introduced. Or, in unique circumstances, a role-playing can take place after reading aloud an entire text. Most dramas, however, involve your reading aloud a portion of text before branching out into a role. This role-playing situation should involve a mode of introduction for new characters. One way to do this is to have the students (in character) interview and introduce each other. In the apartment-tenants' meeting created for the beginning of the "Hey, Al" drama, pp. 81–83, this situation occurs. Remember that you need to model both the role-playing and the introduction of characters' section of each drama.

Do group problem-solving. Guide the drama along until you reach the section of text you have selected for a problem-solving episode. Pose a problem for the new cast of characters to solve. With each drama, vary the type of interaction you request. Consider large-group, small-group, and team efforts. Vary the product of the problem-solving sessions. Structure projects, debates, interviews, written responses, and so on. Share the results of the group problem-solving sessions in a manner that suits the story, as in the list of safety rules in the "Humpty Dumpty" drama.

Focus on character development and interaction. The focus on character development is an integral part of story drama. By asking questions in character roles, you help the students understand point of view, character feelings, conflicts, and character-to-character relationships. Include in your drama action for the "characters." Have the students act out skits, plans of action, pantomimes, and other forms of drama. Body movement and expression add a third dimension to the printed word.

Pose open-ended questions. The next part of drama construction is to focus on an area of text that provides the opportunity to pose open-ended questions. Stop at climactic or thought-provoking parts of the text and pose questions to the group. Prediction plays an important part here. Use different types of questioning techniques: interviewing, student generated questions, clarifying questions such as "Why do you say that?" "Why do you think so?," and so on. Questions can also be used to initiate discussion among groups of students. You and the students will want to consider the answers to these questions from the characters' perspectives.

From *Story Dramas*, published by Good Year Books. Copyright © 1997 Sarah Jossart & Gretchen Courtney.

Written-language responses. Concentrate on incorporating a written-language response into your drama. Students' writing plays an important part in story drama. As a story drama unfolds, students become very involved in the story as well as in the character or role they might be playing. Taking a moment away from this interaction and having the students write gives them the chance to reflect on the story personally, give a personal reaction to a problem or conflict, evaluate their role in the drama, or just take the opportunity to be creative.

Warm-up. Now you are ready to select a warm-up activity that fits with the experience offered by the story drama you created. For example, if your drama involves students in pantomime or movement, you could select a warm-up that involves the students in that type of activity. Remember that poem dramas work very well to get students involved.

Perform and revise the drama. After writing the first draft of your drama, perform it with a group. Your written script is only for organization, planning, and reference purposes. Ad-lib your roles, if you feel comfortable doing so, so you present yourself more clearly as that character. Keep the questioning moving along in the framework of what responses students are giving. The total running time should be between thirty and sixty minutes. Carefully analyze your five basic components: problem to solve, opportunity for multiple-character development, interesting story characters, opportunity for prediction, and enriched vocabulary. What else popped into your head during the drama? What would work better? What parts did students seem to enjoy the most? What questions gave the most opportunity for varied responses? What areas of the drama were difficult for students to understand? Make additions, corrections, variations, and changes. Rewrite and perform the drama again. Your drama should be fluid, adaptable, and creative. It is very likely you will never actually do a drama exactly the same way twice.

Drama Construction Checklist

- Read the entire text.
- Identify story problem(s).
- Plan total running time—between 30 and 60 minutes.
- Create a situation to model role-playing.
- Role-play early in the text.
- Provide student and teacher role-playing opportunities.
- Vary role-playing situations.
- Provide a variety of large-group and small-group activities.
- Include interaction for groups.
- Plan sharing time for groups.
- Vary mode of sharing.
- Establish open-ended questions.
- Use various questioning techniques.
- Incorporate writing activities and extensions.
- Perform and revise the drama using ideas and suggestions that arose during the initial performance.
- Select pre-drama/warm-up activities.

WRITING EXTENSIONS

Writing with story drama is meant to be nonthreatening, short in duration, and not for grading (all student samples shown are first draft). This creates a "safe" atmosphere in which students will choose to write. Of course, you will want to provide time for these writings to be shared if a student wishes to share. You may decide to keep these writings in your students' writing folders. They can be very useful in language arts instruction, when they can be revised or edited according to your instructions. Students feel more ownership when using a piece of their work for follow-up practice, rather than an activity out of a language arts text.

All kinds of writing can be incorporated into story drama. Some writing may be shared writing, when you take dictation, but most often primary students can be asked to do their own writing. Many of our beginning writers may be only putting marks or strings of letters on paper, but they are writing. These writers can "read" their own writings. Collaborative writing is also a nice variation to be considered. In collaborative writing, one piece of writing comes from a small group, with each member of the group contributing to the content of the piece. There is a sense of safety in collaborative writing, and you may wish to consider a collaborative piece with your reluctant writers.

From *Story Dramas*, published by Good Year Books. Copyright © 1997 Sarah Jossart & Gretchen Courtney.

Try to incorporate one of the following ideas into a drama you are preparing. Depending upon the story or poem used, some ideas will work better than others. Also, keep in mind which writing formats your students are familiar with. For example, you should not ask them to write a newspaper article if they have not been instructed in the style of news reporting. Listed below are some writing-activity suggestions.

Write a new ending to a story.

Rewrite a part of the story.

Write a radio advertisement.

Write a job description.

Write recipes.

Write a diary entry.

Write and design greeting cards, such as get-well cards.

Write about fictionalized experiences.

Make all kinds of lists.

Write poetry.

Write letters of all types.

Keep journal entries.

Write newspaper articles.

Rewrite from a different point of view.

Write a daily schedule for a story character.

Write a travel guide.

Write riddles.

Write a text for a mail-order catalog describing the story.

Write a sequel.

Write an advertisement for the book.

Write a song lyric to be sung to a familiar tune.

Write questions you would ask of a story character.

Write your own version of a story.

Write a moral for a story.

INDEX OF STORY DRAMAS

POETRY

Dakos, Kalli. *Mrs. Cole on an Onion Roll.* Simon & Schuster, 1995.

"Mrs. Cole on an Onion Roll"

"Frog–a–lert"

"I Lost My Tooth in My Doughnut"

Hoberman, Mary Ann, sel. *My Song Is Beautiful.* Little Brown and Co., 1994.

"Me," by Karla Kuskin

"I Know Someone," by Michael Rosen

"The End," by A. A. Milne

Moore, Clement C. "A Visit from St. Nicholas."

Singer, Marilyn. *Sky Words.* Macmillan, 1994.

"Skywriting"

"At the Fair"

CONCEPT

Crews, Donald. *Parade.* Greenwillow, 1983.

Hoban, Tana. *A Children's Zoo.* Greenwillow, 1985.

Martin, Bill, Jr., and John Archambault. *Chicka Chicka Boom Boom.* Simon & Schuster, 1989.

Raffi. *Five Little Ducks.* Crown Publishers, 1988.

FANTASY

Fox, Mem. *Koala Lou.* Gulliver Books/Harcourt Brace Jovanovich, 1988.

Goss, Linda, and Clay Goss. *It's Kwanzaa Time!* G. P. Putnam's, 1995.

Graham, Amanda. *Who Wants Arthur?* Gareth Stevens, 1987.

Joyce, William. *Dinosaur Bob.* HarperCollins, 1995.

Komaiko, Leah. *Fritzi Fox Flew in from Florida.* HarperCollins, 1995.

Martin, Rafe. *Will's Mammoth.* G. P. Putnam's, 1989.

Price, Moe. *The Reindeer Christmas.* Gulliver Books/Harcourt Brace, 1994.

Vaughan, Marcia. *Whistling Dixie.* HarperCollins, 1995.

Wood, Audrey. *King Bidgood's in the Bathtub.* Harcourt Brace Jovanovich, 1985.

Yorinks, Arthur. *Hey, Al.* Farrar, Straus and Giroux, 1986.

From *Story Dramas,* published by Good Year Books. Copyright © 1997 Sarah Jossart & Gretchen Courtney.

FICTION

Blos, Joan W. *Old Henry.* WIlliam Morrow, 1987.

Carlstrom, Nancy White. *The Moon Came Too.* Macmillan, 1987.

Hoffman, Mary. *Amazing Grace.* Dial, 1991.

Isadora, Rachel. *At the Crossroads.* Scholastic, 1991

Jaffe, Nina. *In the Month of Kislev: A Story of Hanukkah.* Puffin, 1992.

Marzollo, Jean. *Sun Song.* HarperCollins, 1995.

Mills, Lauren. *The Rag Coat.* Little Brown, 1991.

Rylant, Cynthia. *The Relatives Came.* Bradbury, 1985.

HISTORICAL FICTION

George, Jean Craighead. *The First Thanksgiving.* Philomel, 1993.

Johnston, Tony. *Amber on the Mountain.* Dial, 1994.

Levinson, Riki. *Watch the Stars Come Out.* Dutton, 1985. (Available in Spanish.)

Van Leeuwen, Jean. *Going West.* Dial Books, 1992.

From *Story Dramas*, published by Good Year Books. Copyright © 1997 Sarah Jossart & Gretchen Courtney.

About the Authors

Sarah Jossart's interest in drama began during her elementary school years. White sheets strung on wire with safety pins acted as stage curtains. Desks were pushed together to form seating for relatives and neighbors. In this one room schoolhouse, Sarah and her schoolmates performed. A clearing in the trees formed a kitchen to "cook" mud pies served on plates made from leaves; puppies and kittens dressed in doll clothes were "babies" wheeled around the yard; and a trunk of clothes became a wardrobe for a queen, teacher, and nurse. There Sarah's world of pretending had its beginning.

Besides her interest in drama, Sarah dreams about writing for children. She has taught preschool through graduate level classes and is a Title I Reading Specialist. She lives in Elgin, Illinois, with her husband and two sons.

"The whole world is a stage" is an apt phrase for **Gretchen Courtney's** early years. Every nursery rhyme, story, or experience was repeated to many audiences—often with different endings. Rows of dolls and teddy bears, or at times a patient beagle named Candy, were all she needed to spend many happy hours of invention and creativity. Operas were sung while rocking in the little rocking chair—in rhythm, of course. Camping stories were shared with visiting cousins in the sheltered "wild areas" between the house and porch in suburbia—enlivened with camp stew of nuts, leaves, dirt, and water. It seems that all her life she has been preparing her idea bank so she could share her joy of drama in everyday life with others.

Gretchen works as an educational consultant, having previously taught grades K–8 and served as a district reading consultant. She lives in St. Charles, Illinois, with her husband, son, and daughter.